LEADING BEYOND INTENTION

6 Areas to Deepen Reflection and Planning in Your PLC at Work®

Jeanne **Spiller**   Karen **Power**

Solution Tree | Press
a division of
Solution Tree

555 North Morton Street
Bloomington, IN 47404
800.733.6786 (toll free) / 812.336.7700
FAX: 812.336.7790

email: info@SolutionTree.com
SolutionTree.com

Visit **go.SolutionTree.com/PLCbooks** to download the free reproducibles in this book.

Printed in the United States of America

Library of Congress Cataloging-in-Publication Data

Names: Power, Karen, 1967- author. | Spiller, Jeanne, author.
Title: Leading beyond intention : six areas to deepen reflection and
    planning in your PLC at work / Karen Power and Jeanne Spiller.
Description: Bloomington, IN : Solution Tree Press, [2022] | Includes
    bibliographical references and index.
Identifiers: LCCN 2022001796 (print) | LCCN 2022001797 (ebook) | ISBN
    9781951075453 (Paperback) | ISBN 9781951075460 (eBook)
Subjects: LCSH: School principals. | School management and organization. |
    Educational leadership. | Professional learning communities.
Classification: LCC LB2831.9 .P59 2022 (print) | LCC LB2831.9 (ebook) |
    DDC 371.2/012--dc23/eng/20220331
LC record available at https://lccn.loc.gov/2022001796
LC ebook record available at https://lccn.loc.gov/2022001797

Solution Tree
Jeffrey C. Jones, CEO
Edmund M. Ackerman, President

Solution Tree Press
President and Publisher: Douglas M. Rife
Associate Publisher: Sarah Payne-Mills
Managing Production Editor: Kendra Slayton
Editorial Director: Todd Brakke
Art Director: Rian Anderson
Copy Chief: Jessi Finn
Senior Production Editor: Suzanne Kraszewski
Content Development Specialist: Amy Rubenstein
Acquisitions Editor: Sarah Jubar
Copy Editor: Evie Madsen
Proofreader: Elisabeth Abrams
Text and Cover Designer: Fabiana Cochran
Editorial Assistants: Charlotte Jones, Sarah Ludwig, and Elijah Oates

This book is dedicated to all of the passionate leaders out there doing their best every single day in the service of students. Also, to Dave, Brandon, and Breton for always supporting and loving me no matter what.

—Jeanne Spiller

To Jeanne for accepting my idea to write together and for being my thought partner—you made us better. To my family, Elizabeth, Sandra, Wayne, Bryan, Ryan, Edgar, Kim, and Bonnie—the unconditional love that we have for one another is all that I need. Thank you.

—Karen Power

Acknowledgements

This book represents a continuous learning and writing journey for us as educators, leaders, coaches, authors, and friends. We acknowledge that our unique life and professional experiences complement each other and that without the wonderful opportunities that we have both had to work with educators and leaders in both the United States and Canada, we would not be writing this book.

To you, our readers, thank you. We have appreciated that so many have read and used our first book, *Leading With Intention*: *Eight Areas for Reflection and Planning in Your PLC at Work* ® (2019). We wrote this second book during the global COVID-19 pandemic as we continued to work with schools and districts. Our hearts were warmed and broken, sometimes all in the same day, by the countless examples of courageous, relentless leadership in schools. We felt the exhaustion and frustration of leaders and knew that this book had to support the inner strength that we understand to be critical to leadership success.

We are so blessed to be part of the Solution Tree family. We are grateful for the continuous commitment to student learning and school success that is the foundational work of our professional organization.

Finally, we express our love and gratitude to our families who allow us the space and time to work, even when it is inconvenient to the lives that they have with us. We truly see and appreciate your support.

Solution Tree Press would like to thank the following reviewers:

John D. Ewald
Education Consultant
Former Superintendent,
    Principal, Teacher
Frederick, Maryland

Hector Garcia
Superintendent
District 181
Clarendon Hills, Illinois

Paige Raney
Chair, Division of Education
Spring Hill College
Mobile, Alabama

Steven Weber
Associate Superintendent for
    Teaching and Learning
Fayetteville Public Schools
Fayetteville, Arkansas

Visit **go.SolutionTree.com/PLCbooks** to download the free reproducibles in this book.

Table of Contents

Reproducible pages are in italics.

Chapter 6

About the Authors

 **Jeanne Spiller** is assistant superintendent for teaching and learning for Kildeer Countryside Community Consolidated School District 96 in Buffalo Grove, Illinois. School District 96 is recognized on AllThingsPLC (www.allthingsplc.info) as one of only a small number of school districts with all schools earning the distinction of model professional learning community (PLC). Jeanne's work focuses on the importance and power of strong leadership in schools, of ensuring that *all* students are given the opportunity to learn at high levels, and of standards-aligned instruction and assessment practices. She supports districts, schools, and teams across the United States to gain clarity about and address the four critical questions of a PLC. She is passionate about collaborating with districts, schools, and teams to develop systems for teaching and learning that keep the focus on improving student results.

Jeanne is coauthor of *Collaborating for Success With the Common Core, Yes We Can! General and Special Educators Collaborating in a Professional Learning Community, Leading With Intention: Eight Areas for Reflection and Planning in Your PLC at Work,* and *Help Your Team: Overcoming Common Collaborative Challenges in a PLC at Work* and editor of the *Every Teacher Is a Literacy Teacher* series. She has served as a classroom teacher, team leader, middle school administrator, and director of professional learning.

To learn more about Jeanne's work, follow @jeeneemarie on Twitter.

Karen Power is a consultant and former teacher, principal, superintendent, and senior advisor for professional learning and leadership. Karen has implemented the PLC at Work process both as a principal and superintendent and, for several years as a consultant, she has supported collaborative work in schools to meet the needs of students. Karen is coauthor of *Leading With Intention: Eight Areas for Reflection and Planning in Your PLC at Work* as well as *A Leader's Guide to Reading and Writing in a PLC at Work.* She also contributed to the Canadian edition of *Learning by Doing: A Handbook for Professional Learning Communities at Work* and the anthology *Charting the Course for Leaders: Lessons From Priority Schools in a PLC at Work.*

Karen's work focuses on leadership coaching in schools and districts. She is passionate about growing leaders and improving schools. Karen's international experiences include building collaborative practices through professional learning community (PLC) implementation, district strategic planning, and developing effective instruction, assessment, and evidence-based practices for long-term sustainability.

In 2010, 2011, and 2012, Karen was selected as one of Canada's Top 100 Most Powerful Women in the Public Sector by the Women's Executive Network. She also received the national *Reader's Digest* Leadership in Education Award and was named one of the Outstanding People in the Atlantic Region by Atlantic Canada's *Progress* magazine.

To learn more about Karen's work, visit https://karenpower.blog and follow @power58karen on Twitter.

To book Jeanne Spiller or Karen Power for professional development, contact pd@SolutionTree.com.

Foreword

By Robert Eaker

It's not easy to transform traditional schools into high-performing professional learning communities (PLCs), even under the best of circumstances. Despite the difficulty, many schools and districts have overcome significant obstacles (such as lack of funding, inadequate facilities, and severe poverty within the school community) to successfully implement the processes and practices reflective of a PLC. Overcoming such obstacles takes more time, more focus, and often more resources than in schools that do not face such significant challenges; but it can—and is—being done. It is highly unlikely, however, that any school, from the most affluent to the most economically challenged, can make the PLC transformation in the absence of effective leadership. *Effective leadership is the indispensable factor for reculturing schools.* As powerful as PLC processes are, they are not powerful enough to overcome weak and ineffective leadership.

Recognizing the critical importance of effective leadership is not a new or novel insight. In addition to common sense, research findings from studies of effective schools consistently cite effective leadership as a central requirement for creating effective schools (Hattie, 2009; Manna, 2015; National Association of Secondary School Principals & National Association of Elementary School Principals, 2013; Wallace Foundation, 2013). While there is virtually unanimous agreement on the importance of leadership, there is less agreement regarding what constitutes highly effective leadership practices.

The knowledge base on highly effective leadership practices is expanding, however, and educators and coauthors Jeanne Spiller and Karen Power (2019) have become important contributors, first with their book *Leading With Intention: Eight Areas for Reflection and Planning in Your PLC at Work* and now with this important work, *Leading Beyond Intention: Six Areas to Deepen Reflection and Planning in Your PLC at Work.*

At the core of Spiller and Power's work is the critical understanding that leading others first requires self-reflection and a commitment to self-management. Researcher and author Jim Collins (2001) reminds us that before looking "out the window" and examining the behavior of others, leaders should "look in the mirror" and reflect on their own behavior. While introspection is critical, a conceptual framework for self-reflection enhances the benefits of looking inward. Fortunately, in *Leading Beyond Intention*, Spiller and Power provide both depth and specificity along with excellent tools to enhance leaders' ability to lead beyond intention by leading from within.

This is an optimistic book based on the belief that each of us can enhance our leadership effectiveness. Rather than merely urging leaders to become more effective, *Leading Beyond Intention* provides readers with the tools that can enable not only self-reflection, but more importantly, self-improvement, by guiding readers to reflect on what kind of leaders they are, and the kind of leaders they can—and should—become. As leadership experts Richard DuFour and Robert J. Marzano (2011) remind us:

> Don't ask if you are leading. You are. Don't ask if you will make a difference. You will. The question is, "What kind of leader will you be, and what kind of difference will you make?" (p. 208)

This excellent vehicle for introspection by Spiller and Power will lead you to your personal answer to this question.

References

Collins, J. (2001). *Good to great: Why some companies make the leap . . . and others don't.* New York: Harper-Business.

DuFour, R., & Marzano, R. J. (2011). *Leaders of learning: How district, school, and classroom leaders improve student achievement.* Bloomington, IN: Solution Tree Press.

Hattie, J. (2009). *Visible learning: A synthesis of over 800 meta-analyses relating to achievement.* London: Routledge.

Manna, P. (2015). *Developing excellent school principals to advance teaching and learning: Considerations for state policy.* New York: The Wallace Foundation. Accessed at www.wallacefoundation.org/knowledge-center/pages/developing-excellent-school-principals.aspx on May 29, 2022.

National Association of Secondary School Principals, & National Association of Elementary School Principals. (2013). *Leadership matters: What the research says about the importance of principal leadership*. Alexandria, VA: National Association of Elementary School Principals.

Spiller, J., & Power, K. (2019). *Leading with intention: Eight areas for reflection and planning in your PLC at Work*. Bloomington, IN: Solution Tree Press.

The Wallace Foundation. (2013, January). *The school principal as leader: Guiding schools to better teaching and learning* (Expanded ed.). New York: Author. Accessed at www.wallacefoundation.org/knowledge-center/school-leadership/effective-principal-leadership/Documents/The-School-Principal-as-Leader-Guiding-Schools-to-Better-Teaching-and-Learning.pdf on May 29, 2022.

Introduction

Imagine that it is a beautiful day, and you are out for a drive. You come to a bend in the road. A signpost states, "Courageous, intentional long-term thinking leaders this way. Leaders who want to maintain the status quo, turn the other way." In your mind, you know which direction you want to take; however, you wonder if you take those chances often enough. Do you intentionally seek opportunities for long-term thinking that deepens your work? Or are you more likely to just want to get the job done? In inspirational speaker Simon Sinek's (2019) *The Infinite Game*, the author describes an *infinite game* as one with no finish line, no winning or losing, and the goal is to keep playing, to perpetuate the game. In this game, you are constantly working to improve and create growth opportunities. Sinek (2019) reminds leaders that the opposite, a *finite game*, is about winning or losing, and for most, it is truly about getting to the finish line. When you play the finite game, leadership feels like a race you are running; perhaps you are missing opportunities along the way and just trying to win. During the drive, the signpost represents Sinek's (2019) two directions—choosing the long-term-thinking direction is symbolic of the infinite game; you want to continue to advance the depth of your work with continuous improvement. On the flip side, if you select the direction of maintaining the status quo, you are more apt to play the finite game; you are just getting through the day and to the finish line, which matters most.

As a leader, you choose which direction you take—how your leadership style will take shape. Is it about leading with a finite mindset, when being right and getting to the finish line are more important than the people and processes around you, or are you leading from an infinite mindset, taking the time to build capacity and lead from your heart? The latter style is not about being soft, but the opposite; it is about bravery and dealing with difficult situations as needed. It is about understanding problems and using evidence to improve. We see *grit* (or mental toughness) and bravery every day in schools and districts. We want to celebrate this and help you further develop this skill set. We believe the world needs leaders who are willing to *lead from within* more than ever. Courageous and intentional leadership builds from within yourself; when you can find the grit to improve and seek opportunities to empower and trust.

Along this professional journey, leaders build the skills of others. One process that embraces shared opportunities is the Professional Learning Communities at Work (PLC) process. Through professional collaboration, districts and schools focus on student learning. Leading this work requires a results-driven mindset and deep understanding of how to create necessary cultural shifts. And most importantly, deep implementation of the PLC process happens or *does not* happen, depending on leadership. In fact, we argue that leadership is the number-one determining factor in school success. Leading through professional collaboration and being able to implement necessary changes within a system require the inner strength and courage that this book explores. Whether you are reading this book as a new principal engaging in the PLC process or a district superintendent wishing to advance your own personal leadership skills, consider your impact on others. How persistent are you in leading change, and how tight are your expectations around the mission, vision, values (collective commitments), and goals of your school or district? This matters to others. Developing and sustaining this focus require you to *lead beyond intention*. It is moving beyond words to actions and processes to build a PLC culture and having the *grit* to maintain the direction required despite roadblocks, distractors, and resisters. This is when we truly see leadership from within.

In our first book, *Leading With Intention: Eight Areas for Reflection and Planning in Your PLC at Work* (Spiller & Power, 2019), we asked readers to "move from focusing on you, personally, as the leader, to the intentional practices that guide your work as a school leader" (p. 8). In this second book, we move beyond the intentional practices that guide your work to focus on how readers can lead from within. As leadership coaches, we work to meet leaders where they are in their leadership journey and move them forward. In each situation, the work aligns with the needs of the leader. We wrote this book for you to reflect, identify your strengths, and build on them. We hope you will recognize areas for growth and build on those too. Use the chapters as you need them, as each one provides ample reflective exercises and templates for you to focus on. As you reflect, consider where you are in your PLC journey. Are you where you want to be? If not, why not? Are you leading with intention and focus? Are the practices you want to see implemented happening? Is your leadership moving beyond intentionality to deep alignment with what you value and hold dear as a leader? Since you have read this far into our introduction, we know you want to build your ability to lead from within. In our opinion, people who *lead from within* are leaders who want nothing more than to live their lives according to their truths and on their own terms. They lead from a core level that resides deep within their heart—in a deeply rooted space where their values speak of what is best within them. We both have followed in the footsteps of great mentors and role models. These leaders model leading from within and demonstrate a deep desire to lead with an infinite mindset.

Throughout this book, we invite you to consider how you lead beyond intention. As coaches, we know leadership necessitates both *skill* and *will*, and it is possible to learn to be a more decisive leader. In fact, we acquired many of our abilities to lead and coach through trial and error. As we consult with schools and districts, we observe leaders willing to read, study, practice, and seek coaching. Those we work with every day inspire us as they seize every opportunity to develop more vital skills and expertise. The great news is we know you can learn to lead from within. It takes profound drive and the desire to improve. However, this does not have to be a natural tendency for you; you can foster it.

If being a great leader only demanded *skill*, learning to lead would be a less challenging task. If *skill* is the only requirement, many more success stories would exist, and fewer people would take early exits from leadership roles. However, through experience, we both know the *will*—being able to find the inner strength and resolve to maintain focus, courage, and integrity—is what truly separates strong, impactful leaders from those who merely hold a leadership position.

Throughout this book, we provide examples of real-life situations as well as some fictional scenarios to support the text. Fictional scenarios are based on real situations in real schools, but the school or name of the leader has been changed for anonymity. In either case, they are all from our experiences both as leaders and as coaches and warrant sharing with you.

Focus of This Book

Our first book, *Leading With Intention* (Spiller & Power, 2019), develops a theme of *eight*, with eight chapters and eight reflective exercises at the end of each chapter. *Eight* symbolizes abundance, power, balance, and the ability to make decisions; we focused on the eight areas we believe to be most important to our work as leadership coaches that require PLC leaders to take action. Throughout the book, we focus on leading through an intentional lens as you develop and focus on priorities, shared leadership, communication, instruction, and of course, the students.

In this book, we remain focused on the great need to be intentional in your leadership practices and pay particular attention to what must be done. We aim to add a lens of *will* and deepen your understanding, as a leader, of the requirement to dig deep and lead from inner strength—from within. We remind you that you can learn and strengthen your *will*. This intentional focus will create the synergy and confidence that produce outstanding leadership.

Six Areas

The Pythagoreans acknowledge the number six to be the first perfect number. In mathematics, an *ideal number* is when all the number's divisors (excluding the number itself) are added, and the sum equals the number itself. The number *six* is the symbol of luck, the highest number on a die, and the symbol of Venus, the goddess of love. Having a *sixth sense* refers to extrasensory perception (ESP). It is also common to hear someone using the phrase *the sixth sense* when referring to a hunch or instinct (MysticalNumbers.com, n.d.).

Leading from within requires an abundance of your sixth sense as you learn to understand yourself and others and develop your capacity to trust your instincts to make decisions. Our purpose in writing this book is to help you explore your instincts and tendencies as a leader and consider possibilities and potentially new ways of leading that will guide you as you encounter challenges along the leadership road. We write about the following six areas in this exploration.

1. Bravely leading from within

2. Leading with coaching

3. Leading through conflict and challenge

4. Leading change with accountability

5. Going the extra mile (and looking after yourself)

6. Learning always and from everywhere

Bravely Leading From Within

Courageous leadership is what schools need. Where there are bold, resolute leaders who fiercely stand for what is best for students and uphold this stance no matter what, the school staff are more likely to embrace any change and innovation necessary to improve outcomes for students. Leaders demonstrate brave leadership in their everyday actions. Five brave actions leaders take include (1) defining and protecting values, (2) confronting reality by telling and encouraging the truth, (3) exceptional listening, (4) being reflective, and (5) getting comfortable with leading change and getting messy. Brave leadership is not easy, and it requires leaders to overcome the often formidable obstacles that can get in the way, such as the challenge of making thoughtful decisions and overcoming the desire to be liked. Leaders who recognize the importance of being respected over being liked are more likely to engage in behaviors like telling the truth, even if it's unpopular, and saying "no" when they need to. Brave leadership requires unwavering commitment and self-appraisal. In this first of six areas, we guide your thinking on becoming more reflective, confident, and comfortable as you face obstacles and courageous decisions.

Leading With Coaching

The coaching approach to leadership provides an opportunity to be more in tune with the specific and individual motivations of those you lead. As a leader, you want to develop people who can problem solve and think through options, weighing the pros and cons of each one. As leadership coaches, we aspire to coach more than tell, and do our best to build capacity and potential whenever possible. We also know there are times when we must guide and direct those we lead. As a leader, listen attentively and consider what you know about the person speaking. This is how you begin to understand the direction you want to take as a leader. In this second chapter, you learn to assess whether the person could benefit most from coaching stances including consulting, collaborating, or reflective coaching.

Leading Through Conflict and Challenge

Leading from within tests the patience of every leader we have had the pleasure to work with. Leaders can exacerbate challenging situations and encourage harmful or destructive behaviors in those they lead by simply not addressing them. Expectations in an organization are often more visible by what the leader allows to happen than the leader's officially stated *tights*—the leader's non-negotiable expectations. In theory, leaders would lead and everyone would follow. It takes much more than influence for others to change, and a great place to start is to insist on the expected practice. Leaders build a consensus of collective commitments, acknowledging the need to develop a collective understanding of exemplary work. The change process takes an intentional focus to remove obstacles and resolve resistance. In this chapter, we take you on a journey of one school leader's positive approach to building joint ownership through collective commitments as a way of creating change and leading through conflict and challenge.

Leading Change With Accountability

Leading from within requires the leader to know the score; in other words, there is no hiding from the story the data tell. The best-laid plans—school-improvement plans, district strategic plans, lesson plans, collaborative-team unit plans, and so on—are only worth the paper they are written on unless you model them through actions and expectations, and monitor these expectations for results. Leading change within your system requires intentional, accountable actions. As you build a culture focused on results for students, consider the value of building your staff's knowledge, skills, and dispositions (or *will*) to monitor and respond to student data effectively. Implementing a cultural shift through change includes goal setting and progress monitoring to determine what is working and what is not. Every journey has a beginning, stops along the way, and an end or goal. Leading from within requires a personal commitment to knowing the beginning, monitoring the signs along the way, and understanding the desired outcomes. This chapter builds a deeper understanding of leading change with a focus on accountability.

Going the Extra Mile (and Looking After Yourself)

Leading from within requires intentionally acknowledging a personal commitment to accept the role and responsibility of leadership. As we coach leaders, we witness an authentic desire to remain focused; however, we also experience the struggle that transpires for leaders without the grit to endure. Leaders who practice consistent actions that tightly align to their expectations create synergy, and others follow. Leading from within requires staying the course no matter what and ignoring the seeds of doubt that creep into your thinking. *Developing a thick skin* means you deal with the situations at hand, but as leaders, we make it less about anger, pride, or hurt and more about what will move your school or district forward. We find the most impactful way to balance our work and life is when we emphasize taking care of ourselves. This chapter provides an opportunity to self-reflect and considers strategies to increase a work-life balance and stay strong, and focus on leading from within.

Learning Always and From Everywhere

Leaders who lead from within constantly seek information that allows them to deepen their understanding of leadership and what it takes to lead well. Leadership lessons are all around you naturally in your day-to-day interactions, in the news, in your observations of students, in the actions of other leaders, and in the responses that you witness to your leadership. Think about how you can use these experiences to guide your leadership practice. You will consider the three guiding principles of (1) pursue, (2) personalize, and (3) practice to advance your leadership journey. You will learn how to pursue information that is reliable, useful, compelling, and resonates with you; personalize the data by making meaning of them based on your experiences and context; and practice what you learn by using the information to enhance your work. As you grow and learn as a leader, you will discover it is vital to surround yourself with others who want to lead and learn with you. This chapter shows you how sharing what you know with others solidifies your understanding and possibly provides new ways of thinking about learning.

Reflect and Practice

As you read this book, create time to reflect on your leadership style and the skills you want to grow as you lead from within. Throughout, you will see reflection questions to assist you. Each chapter also invites you to participate actively, using the templates and tools to learn the six actions. Read from beginning to end, or read the chapters in any order, coming back to the ones you need or that inspire you. At the end of each chapter, we suggest leadership actions you can do in six minutes, six weeks, and six months related to each topic, including direct statements about what we believe thoughtful leaders *do* and *avoid* in their practice.

We believe the strength of this book lies in the reflection and application of each reader. We aspire to build on your strengths and inspire you to find the continuous courage to grow both skill and will. We have learned a delicate balance of both makes great leaders, and we invite you to take this journey with us.

Most importantly, throughout this journey, please celebrate! Celebrate what you already do so well, the small and the significant accomplishments that make up the minutes of your day, and how you demonstrate brave, courageous leadership from within. Take care of yourself even when you must give much more than you think you have to give, and always intentionally know your current reality and build relationships as you focus on results. Finally, learn always and from everywhere, beginning with this book.

Chapter 1

Bravely Leading From Within

Leadership is not about titles or the corner office. It's about the willingness to step up, put yourself out there, and lean into courage. The world is desperate for braver leaders. It's time for all of us to step up.

—Brené Brown

Be brave. Show courage. These are two little pieces of advice people often receive during personally and professionally challenging times. *Merriam-Webster's Online Dictionary* defines someone who is *brave* (n.d.) as one with mental or moral strength to face danger, fear, or difficulty. When high-ranking company leaders were asked, "What, if anything, about the way people are leading today, needs to change in order for leaders to be successful in a complex, rapidly changing environment where we're faced with seemingly intractable challenges and an insatiable demand for innovation?" the response was quite simple: "We need braver leaders and more courageous cultures" (Brown, 2018, p. 6). The research participants specifically suggest elements of *bravery* and *courage* when describing successful leadership.

Based on our experiences working in schools, we concur with the research participants' assessment. We have observed that where there are bold, resolute leaders who fiercely stand for what is best for students and uphold this stance no matter what, the school staff are more likely to embrace the change and innovation necessary to improve outcomes for students. Finding the mental strength despite all obstacles and stepping up as needed take courageous personal resolve. Leading from within draws on your inner strength and resilience, and aids you in building confidence in yourself and others. The exceptional leaders we have worked with recognize that determined, empowered teachers are optimal for students, so they mold their school culture with a sharp focus on ensuring their staff feel equipped to contribute courageously to the school mission and vision. As a leader, do everything in your power to help the organization and those you lead become as effective as possible.

This opening chapter investigates the *why* and *what* of brave leadership and courageous cultures crucial for school improvement. Together, let's acknowledge the obstacles that get in the way of leadership impact and how to overcome them. We ask you to reflect and explore strategies and opportunities to develop your style of brave leadership and hear from school leaders about the lessons learned from their experiences.

Coauthors and school-improvement experts Anthony Muhammad and Luis F. Cruz (2019) write:

> Leadership represents the ability to use influence to improve organizational productivity. Leadership is not a position; it is a set of actions that positively shape the climate and culture of the working environment. In essence, leadership is a verb, not a noun. We know a good leader is present when those whom [they influence] have become more effective and productive at their given task because of the impact of the leader. (p. 2)

In our opinion, this requires courage and honesty.

We know it's not easy to be a brave leader. It means you must trust yourself, know what you stand for, embrace fear, be vulnerable, and essentially be unflinching and dauntless. Sounds easy, right? We know it's not, but we also know how powerful it is when we witness brave leaders in action. Leading from within begins with harnessing every bit of courage you have to lead with a consistent, unwavering focus on what you know will make the most significant impact on students. Read the following two excerpts from school principals. Consider the impact of their work on the day-to-day life of a school.

1. Kimberly Miles, principal of East Gresham Elementary School in Gresham, Oregon, demonstrates how one simple, unremarkable interaction required her to courageously say "no" when a "yes" response would have made the person making the request happier. She describes how she had to disappoint a custodian and some students to avoid diminishing the teaching and learning culture of the school:

> Our highly regarded, dedicated custodian of more than twenty-five years often goes over and above what is asked of him, so when he needs assistance, the school community is always willing to support him. One long-held tradition at East Gresham was for the fifth-grade leadership students to stay after breakfast and help the custodian with his extensive clean-up duties. Students loved spending time with the custodian and helping him and their school. Unfortunately, this tradition of helping the custodian meant students were missing ten to fifteen minutes of their ninety-minute literacy block—instruction they needed for their growth in literacy. (K. Miles, personal communication, January 21, 2021)

Like many people, Principal Miles wanted to comply with the custodian's request for support and continue a much-loved tradition that built student confidence and feelings of ownership and connection, but when she stopped for a moment to consider the decision, she quickly realized the tradition diminished the time students had for learning. She went to the custodian, communicated the *why* behind her decision to end the tradition, and reiterated the importance of helping each member of the school community understand *why* a commitment to creating a teaching and learning culture was critical. By explaining *why*, Principal Miles opened the door to discussions about daily tasks and how she and staff could work further on helping students feel appreciated and valued while completing those tasks.

2. Another example comes from Sarah Stobaugh, principal of Morrilton Intermediate School in Morrilton, Arkansas. She sums up *brave leadership*:

> Deciding always to do what is right for those that you serve. It's not walking past a "mistake" and not working to correct it. I know it sounds a bit cliché, but remember your *why* and your purpose and make all decisions based on that. It's being intentional with your time and your words. There have been several moments when as a leader, I could have chosen an easier route for my teachers and myself, but it would have contradicted our purpose. Courageous leadership is always working parallel with your purpose. For example, a teacher new to our school was

struggling with classroom management and instruction. I was spending quite a bit of time in her classroom, and I was feeling anxious that I wasn't able to change her practice as quickly as I would like. One day as I was going by her classroom, I could tell things were not going well. I was tired and frustrated, so I kept walking. Halfway down the hall, I stopped. I realized that I was taking the easy way out; to be a courageous leader focused on my purpose I needed to go back and work with that teacher immediately, so that is what I did. (S. Stobaugh, personal communication, January 11, 2021)

These two principals' stories are powerful because they demonstrate brave leadership embedded in the simple, everyday decisions they make as leaders. This can sometimes be the significant, bold steps; however, it is often the small interactions with others. How you face daily conflicting opinions, challenge yourself beyond your comfort zone, or take on a task or project can pull you far from your comfort zone.

Reflection

Consider a personal situation when you responded bravely. How did it make you feel? How did it help others?

Brave Leadership and Courageous Cultures

Let's consider the following scenario from a fictional high school. While this account is imagined, it is based on conversations we both had with principals in our coaching work. As Principal Boone prepares for a postobservation conference with a teacher, he contemplates the best way to approach the conversation. The teacher struggles with management, resulting in a disorderly and chaotic classroom environment, and data indicate students are not making sufficient progress. Furthermore, the teacher is often resistant to feedback and support. Principal Boone reflects on previous conversations with this teacher, recognizing he has not expressed his concerns and expectations. He remembers measuring his words carefully so as not to upset the teacher. He felt it was essential to preserve the relationship and worried he would never make progress with this teacher if she didn't like him. As he contemplated the upcoming conversation, he realized if he wanted outcomes to change for students, he had to approach the conversation differently than he had in the past. So, Principal Boone made a plan. As he constructed the plan, he felt that familiar pang of uneasiness, anticipating how taxing and uncomfortable the conversation might be. But then he thought about how this conversation and ongoing classroom improvements could change outcomes for the students in this teacher's classroom and those who would become her students in the future, so he listed the elements of his plan on paper.

1. He would be extraordinarily clear about what the teacher needs to improve, provide explicit examples, and discuss the impact on students using student data.

2. He would ask the teacher how he could support her as she improves identified areas, and offer his suggestions for ongoing professional learning.

3. He would describe his expectations for improvement, including his plan to visit the teacher's classroom every two weeks to check in on progress, review student data, and provide continuous feedback and support.

Principal Boone executed the plan as described, despite the numerous times he considered changing it to keep the peace. As he reflected on the meeting, he recalled that it went exceptionally well despite his initial apprehension. At first, the teacher was hesitant and slightly defensive, but she listened carefully to his feedback, revealing appreciation for his clarity and specific examples. She expressed that in the past, feedback was unclear and vague, making it difficult for her to know exactly how to improve. In addition, she commented that she typically received positive feedback. Hence, she presumed she was doing well until she noticed many of her students didn't demonstrate proficiency on team common formative assessments, leading her to begin examining her classroom practices. She communicated that she was happy to have a partner to guide her in making improvements. Overall, Principal Boone acknowledged he had missed opportunities to help teachers improve their practices in his attempt to avoid conflict. He recognized when he offers support coupled with precise, honest, and straightforward feedback, there is more of a chance for teacher improvement and ultimately higher levels of student achievement.

This scenario demonstrates one reason brave, courageous cultures are vital. Had Principal Boone avoided addressing his concerns about the teacher to not upset her, it would be far less likely that the teacher would have improved her practice. Yet another year would pass with another group of students receiving less-than-ideal instruction, with the teacher believing since she had not heard differently, everything was fine. Moments like this one present themselves daily in the life of school leaders.

This one situation, this one conversation may seem insignificant, but each moment matters when building a courageous culture. "Brave unfolds one situation at a time" (Davis, 2018, p. 1). Every day, your staff pay attention to what you do, what you say, and what you don't say and do (Davis, 2018). They will take their cues from you and believe it is OK to behave the same ways you do. You have great power and a heck of a lot of responsibility! If you want to build a brave, courageous culture where people are willing to take risks, you must demonstrate that behavior in your leadership. If you want staff to be direct and clear about what they need, you too must be explicit and transparent in your communications with them. This is true in school leadership, and honestly, in every aspect of life. Leaders model leading from within through the building of a courageous culture, one conversation at a time.

What are the moments that define your leadership? They are everything, and they are everywhere. Stop and think about it. Think about three recent interactions. What did your behavior demonstrate or not demonstrate? Use figure 1.1 to reflect on these moments and how they define your leadership.

List three interactions and reflect on what they demonstrate about your leadership and how they help define it.	
Interaction one:	**What did this behavior demonstrate about my leadership?**
Interaction two:	**What did this behavior demonstrate about my leadership?**
Interaction three:	**What did this behavior demonstrate about my leadership?**

FIGURE 1.1: Reflection—brave leadership interactions.

*Visit **go.SolutionTree.com/PLCbooks** for a free reproducible version of this figure.*

We asked three school leaders to participate in this exercise and include their reflections in the following examples. As you read their stories, think about how these leaders' actions contribute to building braver, more courageous cultures.

Three Brave Leaders

The first leader, Christina Meister, principal of Grace Hill Elementary School in Rogers, Arkansas, shares the following about her reflection.

> As I reflect about the moments that have and continue to define my leadership, there are so many, and you are right—they are everywhere. My leadership is defined by how I choose to spend my time at school. For instance, do I spend my time behind my desk or out in the building? It is defined by the moments I interact with teachers, with students, with parents. My leadership is defined by how I demonstrate my core values and address beliefs and behaviors by both adults and students not aligned with those values. Artifacts such as our master schedule, professional development agendas, and the meeting notes about our conversations show evidence of my leadership. The moments I must make quick *yes* or *no* decisions or just decisions, in general, contribute as well. The good thing is that I also have the opportunity to continue to shape and define my leadership so that the times I make mistakes, the times I say "no" when maybe I should have said "yes," or the times I got more passionately heated than I should have, can be molded and shaped through a lens of more experiences and clearer focus. The moments that define who I am as a leader take place over time. While some of these moments might be pivotal and memorable, most are the ordinary, day-to-day moments that just begin to slowly shape, mold, and define me and what type of leader I will ultimately be known as. I hope that my core values are at the heart of each of those moments and that when I retire, those that worked alongside me know what it is I stood for, what it is I passionately was committed to, and they can say she made a positive difference in the lives of kids. (C. Meister, personal communication, January 18, 2021)

See figure 1.2 (page 16) for a summary of her three interactions.

Principal Meister's three interactions and her reflection on what they demonstrate about her leadership and how they help define it	
Interaction one:	**What did this behavior demonstrate about my leadership?**
Interaction with guiding coalition members about student-achievement data	*My behavior demonstrates a commitment to student learning and collaborative conversations. It also shows my support of the professional learning community (PLC) process and that I value conversations around data.*
Interaction two:	**What did this behavior demonstrate about my leadership?**
Conversation with another principal regarding student-achievement data	*My behavior demonstrates how personally I take it when data are slow to improve. It also shows I tend to see the deficits about where our school is before I can see the growth.*
Interaction three:	**What did this behavior demonstrate about my leadership?**
Observation and follow-up conversation with a teacher	*My behavior demonstrates a focus on student learning, student needs, teacher growth and development, and teacher support.*

FIGURE 1.2: Principal Meister's three interactions.

The second leader, Bob Sonju, principal of Washington Fields Intermediate School in Washington, Utah, shares the following about his reflection.

> When I think of leadership, of course, I naturally begin to think of purpose, vision, and other elements regarding the big picture and how leaders increase the effectiveness of an organization. Terms like *shared leadership*, *school culture*, and *daily climate* seem to always be at the forefront of my thoughts. But I have to be honest, when you posed the question about "moments that define my leadership," I had to think about my last moments that took place today and begin to reframe my thinking about leadership. Although purpose, vision, shared leadership, and other big-picture items are important to leadership, I've learned that leadership is difficult to sum up in terms like these. I believe that leadership is a culmination of the many moments that are presented to us each day. As I consider my last three interactions, I believe they are a glimpse into my thinking

regarding leadership. I truly believe that a person's leadership style is most accurately defined not by the big, stunning display. Instead, those minute-to-minute moments that occur more accurately describe what it is that we most value in our leadership. (B. Sonju, personal communication, January 11, 2021)

See figure 1.3 for a summary of his three interactions.

Principal Sonju's last three interactions and his reflection on what they demonstrate about his leadership and how they help define it	
Interaction one:	**What did this behavior demonstrate about my leadership?**
An interaction with a student who had made not the best choice he could have	*I remember immediately feeling empathy (as I made a few marginal choices growing up) and thinking to myself, "I get it; I've been there. I want to find out your thought process and figure out how to help you learn from this moment." So, I guess I would sum up my leadership style in this particular moment as empathy, understanding, and helping.*
Interaction two:	**What did this behavior demonstrate about my leadership?**
Immediate involvement with a teacher evaluation *Throughout the review, my cell phone was repeatedly notifying me of the multiple texts and calls I was missing. Along with this, my closed glass door only served as a transparent barrier for three separate people who walked by and gave me the "I need to visit with you immediately" look with the accompanying hand gesture. There were times during the evaluation when my attention would drift to wondering about the calls I had missed or what challenges I had in store with the "I need to talk to you" employees.*	*As I drifted between the evaluation discussion with one of my valued educators and all of the items that seemed to be stacking up, I thought, "This moment is important to this educator, so it needs to be important to me." Regardless of the distractions, this colleague needs and deserves my full attention. I finished the evaluation with my very best, singular focus on my colleague's thoughts and ideas. The teacher deserved this. So the leadership style learned from this? People are important and need to feel valued; I need to make sure that I stay true to this principle.*

FIGURE 1.3: Principal Sonju's three interactions.   continued ➔

Interaction three:	What did this behavior demonstrate about my leadership?
With a district specialist about an initiative While reading my emails at the end of a long day, I started to respond to an email when one of the district specialists came in unannounced. Although I hoped this would be a short conversation, I quickly realized it would not be. The specialist wanted to share updates regarding a district initiative. The initiative has been a great one for our school, but the timing of this unannounced visit was cutting into the myriad of items I had left to do before closing the door for the evening. I immediately announced how great it was to see him and how excited I was to hear about the update. Along with this, I also mentioned that I had just ten minutes for the update, and if we didn't finish, I'd love to make an appointment to hear more.	I believe I demonstrated that time is valuable and that setting parameters or boundaries helps manage the day.

The third leader, Donna Arsenault, principal of Edith Cavell School (K–8) in Moncton, New Brunswick, Canada, shares the following observations about her reflection.

> Sometimes, I wonder how I ever got here. Am I leading? Are these people looking at me, Donna Arsenault, for guidance? I ask myself every day, "Am I doing a good job? Am I doing enough for my staff, for our students?" I tell myself the whole imposter syndrome must be real because I pinch myself sometimes thinking, "You can't be the one who these people see as their 'leader!'" And then suddenly, someone says something to me, and I see how and why they see me as a leader. That is a pretty good feeling.
>
> I have always been a sincere person. I show my emotions on my sleeve. I believe that has been both a curse and a blessing through-out my career. I believe showing vulnerability is not a curse. It demonstrates that you are human, that you are honest, that you care, and that you are "one of them."
>
> I asked my vice principal if she could think of a moment that defines my leadership because I just don't see it in me! Without hesita-tion, she gave me three. (D. Arsenault, personal communication, January 8, 2021)

See figure 1.4 for a summary of her three interactions.

Principal Arsenault's interactions (as her vice principal describes) and her vice principal's reflection on what they demonstrate about the principal's leadership and how they help define it	
Interaction one:	**What did this behavior demonstrate about my principal's leadership?**
How you make it your mission to get every student in the classroom an iPad *You sought out community business support to ensure our students all received an iPad. You called on members of the community, hosted a town hall, and asked for support for our students.*	*You are incredibly passionate and dedicated to getting technology in the classroom to prepare students for online learning and ensure students can utilize technology in various capacities. The grant our school received helped with achieving this, but you didn't stop there. You reached out to others by sharing our story and provided even more support.*
Interaction two:	**What did this behavior demonstrate about my principal's leadership?**
Your leadership throughout the COVID-19 pandemic *You created more space and opportunities to meet as a staff informally. For example, you hosted Monday morning greetings with all staff to ensure everyone was returning to school each week understanding the health and safety measures that we were taking during the COVID-19 pandemic. You also checked in with staff and reassured them that we were all OK.*	*Your encouragement to staff at our Monday morning faculty get-togethers just before the holidays was incredible. Morale was low at that time, and you put on your brave face and spoke to the staff very frankly and positively. I think being a leader through the pandemic can come with its own set of challenges, but you have steered our ship fiercely.*
Interaction three:	**What did this behavior demonstrate about my principal's leadership?**
At the beginning of the year, when you fought for the extra teachers and classes *You asked to meet with district staff to discuss the need for additional teachers and smaller classes to accommodate student needs. You knew that there were policies and budget formulas that determined full-time equivalent staff; however, you wanted this to be reconsidered to meet the needs of our school.*	*You know the challenges our teachers and students face very well and understand what they need. Your leadership shone through. You advocated for what we deserved. You also were not afraid to show your vulnerability.*

FIGURE 1.4: Principal Arsenault's three interactions.

As you consider their leadership stories, you can see a clear theme—a deep commitment to students, staff, and decision making that aligns to core values. Principals Meister, Sonju, and Arsenault are vulnerable enough to learn continuously and grow as leaders. They recognize the need to constantly ask themselves, "Could I have reacted differently or approached situations with a different mindset or perspective?" In your work as leaders in schools and districts, it is always best to slow down and think through decisions carefully. Don't just react; take the time to think through your actions. Typically, when you structure your actions through your values, the right moves become clear. Principal Boone took the time to prepare the steps of his plan; he thought the postobservation conversation through carefully. Sometimes, a lack of preparation can cause you to fall back on behaviors not in alignment with your values.

How can you expect others to do what you are not demonstrating in your interactions with them? You must show courage if you want to be more than simply guardians or custodians of your school (Glanz, 2002). The following section will help you identify five key actions you can take toward brave leadership.

Actions Toward Braver Leadership

As you read this section, personally reflect on your actions. Carefully consider how aligned your efforts are to what you truly believe and want to accomplish. Think about brave steps you might take to strengthen this alignment and become more intentional in your actions. For example, as you read the following first action step, *define and protect values*, you may conclude you are crystal clear on the values but not always consistent in preserving those values in your decision making. You may decide to pay close attention to this alignment in your work for several weeks. In our work, we find this type of reflective leadership essential to continued improvement. As leaders, we have both faced complicated decisions that required us to consider our values and use those values to determine the best way to proceed. Unfortunately, we did not always make decisions with our values in mind. It is easy to get caught up in the emotion and want to make a decision that will make most people happy, and we have both been there and regretted it. As you work through the following actions, be honest with yourself, celebrate your strengths, and decide what you will improve.

Brave Action One: Define and Protect Values

When you are clear about what you value, you can protect it. If you are unclear about what you value, then your decision making is typically inconsistent because it isn't attached to anything. Do you have a clear mission, vision, and set of values? If not, start there. Get clear about what you value (personally and in your work) and truly live it in every decision you make as a leader. Support collaborative teams and individuals in doing the same. Make your mission, vision, and values more than just a sign you hang in the hallway. Expect that team and individual actions will align with the mission, vision, and values, and guide teams in making aligned decisions. When staff pose questions like, "Can we give less-complex questions to students we know will not be able to answer the grade-level questions, so they feel success-ful?" respond with, "If we make that decision, how does it align with our mission statement of high levels of learning for all students and our value of high expecta-tions for all?"

In a supportive and respectful way, guide the conversation back to beliefs and values, and support the team in thinking through other ways to address their con-cern. When the leader consistently reinforces this, teams and individuals will soon stop asking these types of questions because they know the response. When leaders are inconsistent, these types of questions keep coming because it is possible that maybe, depending on the day, they might get an answer that allows them to operate outside the system's values. Doing this can sometimes cause teams or individuals whose values don't align with the school's to go covert. Teams or individuals may not pose questions to the leader because they know the response and may covertly take action misaligned with the mission and values. This is why leaders must pay attention to what is happening with teams. This does not necessarily mean leaders must attend every team meeting. Still, it does mean leaders must check in often with teams, ask to see artifacts, review team meeting minutes, and respectfully hold people accountable and correct the situation when the leaders discover misalign-ment. Brave leaders pay attention to what is happening in their schools and address it directly and honestly.

Yes, it is much easier not to know or pretend not to know so you don't have to address what could be a difficult conversation, but is that the type of culture you want to create? Have the courage to respectfully address those who do not follow through on the commitments and hold yourself accountable for modeling the behaviors you expect of others. To protect the values of a system, confronting reality, speaking the truth, and encouraging the truth from others are necessary. Brave action two pursues this topic.

Brave Action Two: Confront Reality, Say the Truth, and Encourage the Truth

You absolutely cannot make a series of good decisions without first confronting the brutal facts (Collins, 2001). When the facts are clear and confirmed, it is easier to know which way to proceed. When the facts are hazy or unconfirmed, well, it is easier not to act at all. Brave leaders want to know what is happening; they seek information to address what is happening. For example, a principal has a suspicion that one of the schools' collaborative teams has not been administering the team common formative assessments (CFAs), and therefore, has not been examining the data together, even though the principal distinctly communicated this expectation. Brave leaders will verify that their suspicion is accurate, discern why the team is making the decision, reiterate why CFAs and team data discussions are essential, support the team in moving toward the expectation, and hold the team accountable by attending meetings and monitoring the team's work until the team is consistently and effectively implementing the expectations. Will there be awkward and uncomfortable moments in this series of events? Absolutely, but the alternative is to avoid the truth and allow the team to continue functioning out of alignment with expectations and values. What does this communicate to the other teams? It is likely to convey the leader's lack of commitment to the school's mission and values and the message that expectations and values are simply suggestions and not upheld by the leader. We see this often in our coaching work with leaders who wonder why teams are not embracing the PLC process. The conversation usually goes something like the following.

> **Principal:** I can't get them to see the value in the PLC process. They say they don't have time to review the data together.
>
> **Coach:** Do you know what they are spending their time doing during collaborative meetings?
>
> **Principal:** They say they are planning lessons together.
>
> **Coach:** Do they know how students are responding to the instruction they have already provided, and are they adjusting their plans accordingly?
>
> **Principal:** I am not sure. I should probably find out.
>
> **Coach:** Yes, you must find out to communicate the importance of the process and help them as they work to implement it. When teams plan without the benefit of the student data, they are not focused on learning; instead, they are focused only on teaching. A focus on learning is one of the

big ideas of a PLC. The next step is to meet with the team to discuss the
importance of CFAs and data discussions to guide instruction. Work with
them to confront the obstacles and find a way to successfully add CFAs and
data discussions to their planning process.

Honest, truthful conversations like this previous one can be awkward and uncomfortable, but as PLC coaches, we know principals need to have them to effectively lead their teams. The same is true for all school leaders. They must speak the truth with teams because the key to improved student achievement is moving beyond an individual teacher looking at his or her classroom data. It takes same-grade or same-course teacher teams to meet, analyze the results of each interim assessment to understand what concepts in the curriculum are posing difficulty for students, share ideas, figure out the best interventions, and follow up in their classrooms (Christman et al., 2009).

Speaking the truth as a leader is imperative, but so is encouraging others to be honest with you and tell you what is happening and why there is resistance or lack of commitment. When you encourage constructive dissent and healthy debate, you reinforce a team's strength and demonstrate that a better answer lies in the tension of diverse opinions (Tardanico, 2013). Exceptional listening skills underlie the effectiveness of encouraging truthful two-way conversations. Brave action three addresses the concept of great listening.

Brave Action Three: Be an Exceptional Listener

People often underestimate the power of exceptional listening. When leaders pay close attention to what individuals say, they are more likely to soundly understand others' perceptions and opinions. Armed with sound understanding, leaders can ask bold, frank questions to guide people to more optimal answers or solutions.

In our own experiences as school and district leaders, we recognize how extraordinarily busy school leaders are. Finding the space to listen without distraction is difficult. We have watched leaders talk with staff while staring at their computer screens or checking their phones, undeniably missing the opportunity to connect authentically. Brave leaders appreciate authentic connections because they build trust and pave the way for leaders to be honest with people and have hard conversations when they need to. So, how can leaders listen more effectively and truly make connections with those they lead? We suggest the following three actions.

1. **Look people in the eye:** Move anything that could distract you from the conversation out of your line of sight so that you can focus exclusively on the person you are speaking with. Figure out what works best for you to stay in the conversation and not get distracted. Be disciplined in providing an environment that will allow you to stay focused. Staying focused can be difficult for leaders; leaders must consciously commit to staying truly connected with staff. When the leaders' focus is high, so is the likelihood that they can deeply understand others and move to the honest conversations that might be necessary during that discussion or possibly at a later discussion (Turkle, 2015).

2. **Create space in your day so you can give people your full attention:** Intentionally create space in your day for spontaneous conversations. Block off time in your daily schedule to have conversations; in other words, do not make your daily schedule so tight that you cannot naturally spend time building relationships and having conversations. Think about it; has there ever been a day where those unscheduled conversations did *not* happen? Probably not, so do your best to plan for them. There will undoubtedly be days where this is simply impossible. On those days, schedule the conversation when you can listen deeply and focus on the exchange. When you rush conversations, it is less likely to result in meaningful decisions or next steps (Turkle, 2015). In addition, don't feel like you must solve every problem that comes to you during these interactions. Seek clarity about the situation the person has brought to you by asking them questions like, "Why is this a problem for you?" "What would you like to see happen?" and "How can I support you?" Chapter 2 (page 37) contains reviews of these questions in more detail. Another great leadership habit is to create time on collaborative team agendas for leadership feedback and conversation. Too often we see tight agendas that end very abruptly when the bell rings. Allow for time to be built in for feedback to the team about the meeting or coaching conversations and reflection.

3. **Listen for what is *not* said:** Pay close attention to what is happening beyond what the person is saying. What is the person's body language

telling you? Does the person seem nervous, upset, or stressed? This will give you clues about how to proceed with the conversation. If the person appears anxious, it is a clue to good listeners that they need to make the person feel more comfortable and communicate in a calm, relaxed manner. It is best to de-escalate (and not escalate) any of the emotionality you notice.

Intentionally focus on your listening skills for a day. What did you notice? Was it challenging to stay focused on the conversation? Did you look the speaker in the eye? What about finding time to listen? Did it feel like you wanted to focus, but you were thinking about another meeting about to start, so you had to rush things along? How aware were you of the nonverbal cues? Did these cues help you guide the conversation? This type of reflection (specifically focused on one aspect of your leadership) can significantly impact your leadership effectiveness. Brave action four precisely addresses reflection.

Brave Action Four: Be Reflective

Reflection is necessary in all aspects of a leader's role. Reflect carefully on the conversations and decisions you made throughout the day. Consider whether you were truly focused on those you spoke with and the conversations you had. In addition to paying attention to your listening skills (as brave action three addresses), think about your reactions. Did you react and respond in a respectful, honest, and straightforward way? What decisions did you make? Could you have handled any of the conversations or decisions differently, and if so, what actions will you take to correct the situation? In chapter 7 of our first book, *Leading With Intention*, we offer a reflective template for seeking understanding when communicating with others (Spiller & Power, 2019). Using this template (see figure 1.5, page 26), reflect on your current situation or problem that improved communication could impact, specifically, how to clarify the situation or problem and what steps or actions you can take to improve the situation or problem. Throughout that book and this one, we emphasize the importance of reflective thinking as a leader. Leading from within requires you to take the time to be thoughtful. We strongly encourage this practice in all of our coaching sessions.

Current Situation or Problem That Improved Communication Could Impact	What has been done so far to clarify the situation or problem?	What steps or actions could you take to improve the situation or problem?
Mr. Shaw is avoiding my request to meet with parents of one of his students. When I talked to him about this, he was adamant that he could not meet with them because they made him feel bullied. This conversation frustrated me, and I did not seek clarity on why he felt that way.	I have not followed up.	I need to speak with Mr. Shaw again and ask him why he feels bullied by these parents. I will acknowledge his feelings, seeking clarity, and work with him to find a solution. I will offer to host the meeting with the parents if necessary.
The sixth-grade collaborative team is not implementing the PLC process with fidelity. Whenever I meet with them about this, they use time as their reason for not creating common formative assessments or taking the time to dig deep into their student data.	I have attended their meetings, actually taking over one of them to model how the process should look when you use common formative assessments and the evidence from them to discuss student needs. Unless I am there leading the discussion, this work does not continue.	I will meet with them again to seek clarity on why this work is not being done. I want to understand if they do not know how to follow the process, if they don't understand why it is important, or if they are not being compliant with tight expectations. Once I understand, I will create a plan with them to ensure they implement this work with fidelity.

Source: Spiller & Power, 2019, p. 142.

FIGURE 1.5: Reflection—seeking understanding.

*Visit **go.SolutionTree.com/PLCbooks** for a free reproducible version of this figure.*

Brave Action Five: Get Comfortable With Leading Change and Getting Messy

No matter how hard you try to affect win-win decisions, you will not make everyone happy. Knowing you gave your absolute best effort to influence a situation to ensure it is agreeable to both parties makes it easier to live with decisions that do not please everyone. Having a framework of guiding questions to follow can help with those hard-to-make decisions. We find these five questions helpful in clarifying problems and identifying possible solutions.

1. What is the absolute best decision for both sides?

2. What are the long-term effects of the best decision?

3. How would I respond if I only knew the problem and not the people?

4. What decision is consistent with what I believe?

5. What will be the long-term effects of my decision?

Through this questioning process, principals can define each issue with greater clarity, strengthening their courage to make difficult decisions.

In fear-based environments, it's all about protecting the status quo. Envision a better way, a better solution, a better product—and approach it with determination and an open mind, knowing it will be messy and that a midcourse correction may be necessary. Remember, to engage staff, you need to foster them through the change process.

Getting comfortable with your role requires unwavering commitment and self-appraisal. You need to know and expose your most authentic self. It requires action in the face of the unknown and compassion in the face of frustration. It requires an awareness of the impact you're having and a surrender of control that may feel next to impossible. You need to step out of the quagmire of your fears and move forward when that's the last thing you want to do. It requires you to be brave. Figure 1.6 considers the five brave actions and reflects on how you can apply them to your leadership style.

Brave Actions	Current Reality What are you currently doing that reflects this brave action?	Moving Forward What will you do differently to create brave leadership actions?
Brave action one: Define and protect values		
Brave action two: Confront reality, say the truth, and encourage the truth		
Brave action three: Be an exceptional listener		
Brave action four: Be reflective		
Brave action five: Get comfortable with leading change and getting messy		

FIGURE 1.6: Leader reflection—five brave actions.

*Visit **go.SolutionTree.com/PLCbooks** for a free reproducible version of this figure.*

Obstacles That Get in the Way of Being Brave

As we continue our leadership study, it is apparent that brave leadership is not easy; it requires leaders to overcome the often formidable obstacles that can get in the way. It's about how leaders see obstacles. Do leaders see them as opportunities, or do they see them as reasons they cannot proceed? Talk show host, television producer, actress, author, and philanthropist Oprah Winfrey defines the way we suggest leaders approach obstacles: "When you meet obstacles with gratitude, your perception starts to shift, resistance loses its power, and grace finds a home within you" (as cited in Taylor, 2018). We will examine two obstacles that, in our experience, often get in the way of brave leadership—time and wanting to be liked.

Time

In schools, and likely in most workplaces, it seems people are constantly rushing around trying to get things done. Most days feel like a whirlwind of decisions and interactions with students, staff, parents, and other leaders. This whirlwind often propels leaders to make decisions quickly, and sometimes leaders do not carefully consider quick decisions like when they take the time to think through a decision deliberately. We suggest you practice slowing things down a bit so you don't get caught up in the whirlwind. Why slow things down? Slowing down creates time to consider your options and think through the best choice for your students and staff. When rushed for time, you might make a decision that resolves an issue quickly to check it off your list instead of the more courageous choice. We can think of many times when we got sucked into the whirlwind as leaders and regretted the message we inadvertently sent to our staff by making a decision not aligned with our school or district core values. As a district leader, Jeanne often faces decisions that need a quick answer or response. Early in her career, she would jump quickly to the response without thoroughly thinking through all options. Now, she makes a conscious decision to slow things down a bit (well, as much as possible) to use the team around her to consider options and run decisions through a pros-and-cons process, as well as a check to see that the decision options align with her district's values and beliefs.

Best-selling coauthors and brothers Chip and Dan Heath (2013) explore how to improve the quality of decisions in their book, *Decisive: How to Make Better Choices in Life and Work*. One of the most significant decision-making mistakes they address is people's propensity to make decisions too abruptly. They suggest that people consider a few alternatives before making a decision. In a discussion with Lillian Cunningham (2013) as part of her *Washington Post* blog *On Leadership*, Chip Heath suggests there could be more than one way to address the situation.

> Before you make any changes, consider a couple alternatives. We tend to act in a way that psychologists call 'confirmation bias.' Information that is consistent with our initial hypothesis—that supports what we initially believe—is just more readily available and more attractive to us. So what I would say is take the time to look for reasons you might be wrong as well as reasons you might be right.

This process is similar to the one Jeanne and her team employ (see page 28). The key is to slow things down whenever possible; otherwise, it is very easy to fall out of alignment with your values and inadvertently send inconsistent and confusing messages to your staff.

Wanting to Be Liked

"If you just set out to be liked, you would be prepared to compromise on anything at any time . . . and you would achieve nothing!" former British Prime Minister Margaret Thatcher said in May 1989 on the 10th anniversary of her premiership (Press Association, 1989). When your mission is to be liked, you may compromise doing what is right to avoid conflict. This poses a real challenge for those who lead. As leaders, we have experienced the pull between doing the right thing and doing what we think will make people happy. Early in our careers, we admit to making the mistake of choosing the popular decision rather than the decision more aligned to our values. What do you think your tendency is? How do you know? Take a look at the chart in figure 1.7 (page 30). The left side of the chart reveals the behaviors present when you lead from wanting to be liked. The right side of the chart indicates the behaviors more inclined to be present when you recognize the importance of being respected over the need to be liked (Riegel, 2018). Leading from within requires actions and decisions aligned to respect, integrity, and honesty rather than the desire to be popular. What steps can you take to create more opportunities to lead from the right side of figure 1.7?

Professionals and leaders who want (and often need) to feel liked tend to:	Professionals and leaders who recognize the importance of being respected—with or without being liked—are more inclined to:
• Seek positive attention and approval • Engage in gossip rather than giving direct feedback • Try to please everyone • Make promises they can't keep • Keep strong opinions to themselves • Flood people with credit, compliments, and praise • Play favorites (but pretend they don't) • Use information as leverage, withholding or giving it away • Give people tasks they enjoy rather than assignments that stretch and challenge them • Focus more on how people feel (in general, and about them personally) than about achieving outcomes	• Tell the truth, even if it's unpopular • Explain their thinking behind the difficult decisions they make • Acknowledge "the elephant in the room," even if they can't fix it • Say "no" when they need to • Be open-minded and decisive • Give credit when it's due to others and also take it when it's due themselves • Tolerate feelings of disappointment, frustration, sadness, and anger in themselves and others • Hold people accountable for their results • Be consistent and fair in setting rules and expectations • Set and honor boundaries for themselves and others • Deliver negative feedback directly and promptly • Ask for feedback regularly and then act on it • Apologize when they make mistakes and then move on • Model the behavior they expect from others (Riegel, 2018)

FIGURE 1.7: Leading through a lens of popularity versus from alignment to values.

The following is an example of Karen leading from the right side of figure 1.7. This story illustrates leadership that focuses on getting respect versus being liked. As you read Karen's story, think about the obstacles she faced, how she handled each one, and how the story might have had a different ending if she let the obstacles get in the way of what she knew was the right thing for students and staff.

When Karen was superintendent of a school district, she faced a tough decision. One Sunday morning early in the school year, she received word that one of her high schools (housed in a historical building in the downtown core of the city) had been assessed with structural issues; safety experts recommended she close the school immediately. Instantly, Karen faced several obstacles—one was obviously to ensure the safety of students and staff while determining a way for learning to continue. The second immediate obstacle was a logistic and communication plan. This closure would impact many families and staff, including community members who held the historical building near and dear to their hearts. The school board and provincial government officials would need to be well informed and supportive of the action plan. Lastly, she didn't have time to waste as her leadership team needed to mobilize quickly to find space and move students and staff with careful attention to detail.

Karen's leadership team planned to house the 1,500 students in two other buildings—one was a new school scheduled to open in a few weeks, but had not opened yet. The other required moving students from one elementary school to another with low enrollment to create space for half of the high school to take over the first school. The high school students were split; there was no other way to continue the school year. Over the weekend, furniture was moved, and the new temporary schools reopened in a week. Karen and her leadership team felt they made the best decisions throughout this journey, focusing on safety as the priority. However, initially, the decision upset both high school and elementary parents. The media, unfortunately, sided with the parents. Karen and her team faced very hostile public meetings fueled by negative media coverage. Initially, it seemed the shock of the quick and immediate decision to close the school and move students upset parents and the community. As the year went on, the parents saw that school and learning continued with little disruption and students, staff, and families adjusted to the change. However, the community at large feared the long-term closure of a historic building in the heart of the city. The alumni of the school continued to lead a public campaign against the closure of the school despite the health and safety issues. This was a constant obstacle despite her and the staff's belief that they provided a safe solution to a problematic situation. There was no economical or easy fix to the structural issues, and Karen decided this was best for the students and staff. On many occasions, Karen had to justify her decision to government officials and the public while working diligently to operationalize and ensure a smooth transition to the new learning environments for all students.

Over time, the school board closed the building permanently and built a new high school for the students. Looking back now, Karen knows this was one of the most challenging times in her career. She felt vulnerable throughout the debates and did not appreciate the lack of public support. There were many times when Karen and her leadership team doubted their own decision and sound judgment; however, they knew that the brave decision to close was the right one, despite public opinion. The views of others, difficult operational situations including space, bussing, and, of course, finances, created obstacles. As Karen found out, leadership isn't a road to popularity, but bravely putting students first is always the right decision.

> ### Reflection
>
> Keep it real. Consider a time when you knew that you allowed an obstacle to get in the way of courageous leadership. What could you have done differently?

Wrap-Up

As former First Lady Rosalynn Carter once said, "A leader takes people where they want to go. A great leader takes people where they don't necessarily want to go but ought to be" (BrainyQuote, n.d.). Be brave enough to survey staff and ask them what they need from you as a leader. Be vulnerable and listen to their feedback and adjust accordingly. If you interview staff, you must be willing to do something with the information you receive, or it is not worth asking for it. You will be modeling what it looks like to be vulnerable and brave. This is how you create a courageous culture; leading from within means that you will gather the courage to make many decisions—decisions that may not always be popular. In this chapter, we ask you to consider what holds you back. We explored some reasons, including being held back by anxiety and fear that people will not like you. Leaders often stumble when they don't take the time to consider their options before jumping into decisions. The bottom line is brave leaders confront what they need to confront. They have straightforward conversations they need to have. They balance willpower and patience to take on the issues, take risks, engage vulnerabilities, and remain steadfast in addressing behavior not aligned with the school or district value system.

We ask you to consider what you stand for. Are you consistent? Do you always stand your ground regarding what you believe? Courageously espouse your beliefs and live them wholly. Run through all decisions to ensure alignment with values. Do not waver. Use the reflective tool at the end of this chapter (see page 34) to consider your next brave steps. In chapter 2 (page 37), we explore the fine art of coaching others. Leading from within includes developing and empowering others through coaching. We explore how you can develop these skills as a leader.

Six-Sentence Summary

Where there are bold, resolute leaders who fiercely stand for what is best for students and uphold this stance no matter what, the school staff are more likely to embrace the change and innovation necessary to improve outcomes for students. Leaders demonstrate brave leadership in their everyday actions. Five brave actions leaders take include defining and protecting values, confronting reality by telling the truth and encouraging the truth, exceptional listening, being reflective, and getting comfortable with leading change and getting messy. Brave leadership is not easy, and it requires leaders overcome the often formidable obstacles that can get in the way, like overcoming the desire to be liked. Leaders who recognize the importance of being respected over being liked are more likely to engage in behaviors like telling the truth, even if it's unpopular, and saying "no" when they need to. Brave leadership requires unwavering commitment and self-appraisal.

Making an Impact in Six: Bravely Leading From Within

The following six ideas provide opportunities for further reflection and action. We provide three reflections on what great leaders do and avoid doing to gain focus, as well as three considerations for how to make an impact in six minutes, six weeks, and six months to guide your leadership planning and practice.

Thoughtful Leaders Do . . .	Thoughtful Leaders Avoid . . .
1. Recognize that clear, honest communication is critical and engage in brave conversations by professionally addressing actions not aligned with the organizational values.	Prioritizing keeping the peace and preserving relationships over ensuring that actions align with espoused organizational values
Current reality and next steps:	
2. Listen profoundly and thoroughly when in conversations with people throughout the day.	Allowing distractors to claim their focus while in conversations with people
Current reality and next steps:	
3. Reflect on interactions that occur throughout the day. Reflections focus on how interactions reflect brave, courageous leadership and areas for improvement.	Moving through each day on autopilot without taking the time to stop and reflect
Current reality and next steps:	

4. What will you do in six minutes to be a braver leader?

For example:

At the end of each day, take six minutes to write down all of the interactions you can recall. Consider how you demonstrated brave leadership and ways in which you could have been more courageous.

My ideas:

5. What will you do in six weeks to be a braver leader?

For example:

Once per week for six weeks, observe another leader in interactions with staff. Let this leader know you are observing to learn and improve. Focus on how the leader demonstrates courageous leadership.

My ideas:

6. What will you do in six months to be a braver leader?

For example:

Once per week for six months, interview a staff member, asking what he or she needs from you as a leader. Ask what the staff member appreciates about your leadership and how he or she thinks it could improve. Incorporate the feedback into your leadership actions moving forward.

My ideas:

Chapter 2
Leading With Coaching

Each person holds so much power within themselves that needs to be let out. Sometimes they just need a little nudge, a little direction, a little support, a little coaching, and the greatest things can happen.

—Pete Carroll

Coaching—that word holds different meanings depending on people's personal experiences. Educators may have been coached as an athlete, or experienced instructional coaching as a teacher or leadership coaching as a building or district leader. Perhaps their only familiarity with coaching has been as a spectator at a sporting event. No matter what people's experiences are, they form an opinion based on the quality of those experiences. How the coach approached the coaching process likely influenced your perceptions and how you define what coaching is. Before moving into deeper conversations regarding the actual process and power of coaching as a leader, we will be distinct about our definition of *coaching*. As we considered our interpretation of *coaching* for this chapter, we explored myriad meanings. We were struck first by the sheer number of definitions that exist and heartened by the one unifying focus present in all of them—*unlocking human potential*.

Our definition of coaching embodies the quote that opens this chapter by Seattle Seahawks head coach Pete Carroll. As a football coach, the context in which Carroll coaches is different from an educational setting, but can certainly apply to the work of educators. Coach Carroll says it simply and clearly—*let out the power within individuals, providing direction, support, and coaching so great things can happen.* This philosophy is further illustrated in Carroll's work with Michael Gervais, a sports psychologist. Gervais describes the philosophy guiding interactions with the athletes comprising the highly successful Seahawks football program:

> We see every day as an opportunity to compete and be the best ver-
> sion of yourself. Being more present on a daily basis as you engage
> with whatever you do alongside society as a whole. Relentlessly
> competing to be your best self is an extremely rewarding process.
> (as cited in Schottey, 2013)

This is what we believe great leaders do when they lead from within—work to assist those they lead to greatness. The coaching approach to leadership provides an opportunity to be more in tune with the specific and individual motivations of those you lead. In turn, this contributes to more profound insight into your school or district, the challenges you face, and how you might resolve them. Throughout this chapter, we focus on using coaching strategies to achieve this purpose as a leader. As leadership coaches, we both aspire to *coach more than tell* and do our best to build capacity and potential whenever possible. We also know there are times when we must guide and direct those we lead. Use this chapter to reflect and explore your coaching style as a leader, and how you can embed more of these practices as you lead from within.

Reflection

What is your view of coaching? What has shaped the beliefs you hold? How does this impact your daily focus?

Consider this second definition of *coaching* from Sir John Whitmore (2017), a pioneer in the executive coaching industry: "Unlocking a person's potential to maximize their own performance. It is helping them to learn rather than teaching them" (p. 8). This definition provides another connection to *unlocking potential*. It implies that coaching is not simply what leaders teach or when they provide answers but instead how they facilitate and support individuals in finding their own solutions—empowering them to discover answers and build capacity to do more of that, on their own, in the future. In other words, it is not productive to create an environment where staff need or rely on a direct answer from the leader to determine the next steps. As a leader, you want to develop people who can problem solve and think through options, weighing the pros and cons of each.

Brave leaders do not merely aspire to compliance; they don't want staff saying "yes" to everything and anything. Doing this creates a culture where the norm is to come to the leader for the answers and then doing exactly what the leader says. This is *not* coaching.

As you begin to explore how you can lead more from a coaching mindset, consider this example. A teacher approaches you asking for guidance on how to handle a difficult situation with a student; instead of providing the answer, you coach or guide the teacher through a series of questions to help explore options and his or her own thinking first. As leaders, we guide the response based on the questions we ask. Simply starting with "What do you think?" and then probing further for more information will help you deeply understand what drives the teacher's thinking. This interaction will lead to the individual feeling empowered and help him or her consider how to react to similar situations in the future. If you simply provide an answer, the opportunity for empowerment and unlocking potential is lost. The great benefits of coaching as a leadership style include the learning opportunities inherent in the coaching process that are not present when you merely tell people what to do or what direction to take. For example, there is the opportunity to foster thinking, reflection, and actions that align with the espoused values of the school or district. A busy teacher, for instance, may not consider that the district's mission and vision impact his daily classroom actions. As a leader, you also have an opportunity to coach with an equity lens, ask questions, and lead discussions that aid teachers in unearthing unintentional bias or prejudgments about students and their learning.

To clarify, we haven't derived our own new definition of coaching. Instead, we focus on the unifying theme we notice in so many of the descriptions we explore, unlocking human potential. Leaders committed to helping those they lead unlock their potential so students, schools, districts, and ultimately, humanity reap the reward of empowered, knowledgeable, and focused educators. This unifying theme shapes the ideas, protocols, and processes in this chapter. As discussed earlier, this theme implies that whenever possible, leaders facilitate and support individuals in finding their own solutions—empowering them to discover answers and build capacity to do more of that, on their own, in the future. However, there are times when this coaching style may not be the best initial option. It may be necessary to provide more direct leadership or work side by side to model expectations to truly unlock human potential. Let's explore the three leadership stances of consultant (more direct leadership), collaborator (side by side), and reflective coach, and how the three stances are useful leadership styles of coaching in the quest to empower your staff.

Three Leadership Stances

What does it look like when leaders include elements of coaching in their leadership practices? Leading from within requires you to know when to coach and when you need to take a more direct approach. This is often the most challenging part—knowing what practice is necessary. However, the key is integrating coaching elements to focus on unlocking potential and developing empowered staff. When principals take a coaching approach, they incorporate some aspects of coaching when appropriate into the different conversations they have, even if those conversations are not actual coaching conversations (Campbell & van Nieuwerburgh, 2018). As we take a deeper look into leading with elements of coaching, it is vital to start the discussion with a focus on listening. In chapter 1 (page 9), we discussed actions leaders can take to be more daring and braver as leaders. Brave action three refers to being an exceptional listener. It is a brave leadership action because deep listening requires vulnerability and, most importantly, communicates your interest in people and their perspectives. It allows you to understand another's context fully and focus on helping the person find a solution, avoiding doing the problem solving for him or her. This forges more authentic connections and allows the leader to fully understand and respond precisely to each person's needs. Vulnerability is at play here, as you are not controlling the conversation and have no idea where the conversation will take you.

Coauthors Laura Lipton and Bruce M. Wellman's (2017) three mentoring stances (consultant, collaborator, and coach) can be useful when approaching conversations with your staff. While Lipton and Wellman (2017) present these stances in the context of mentoring, we apply them here through the lens of leadership. As a leader, listen attentively and consider what you know about the speaker as you begin to understand the direction you want to take. You will reflect and learn whether the person could benefit most from consulting, collaborating, or reflective coaching. As you read about the three stances, consider your current leadership style. Is one of these stances more common in your practice? How can you develop a more well-rounded approach to leading from within?

Consultant Stance

A leader might determine a person could benefit from direct advice because the person is new to the teaching profession or new to the position, deciding the consultant stance is the most appropriate. Figure 2.1 shows the leader more prominently since he or she takes on a more significant part of the thinking and contribution. In this stance, the leader may offer knowledge or expertise to the conversation. For example, a middle school principal in a conversation with a teacher who transferred to the middle school after teaching second grade for many years might decide to give straightforward advice regarding the teacher's question about ongoing negative behaviors students demonstrate in the classroom. The principal may say things like, "Here's how I like to think about situations like that" or "In my experience with middle school students, this strategy has been effective." Another situation that may engage a leader in the consultant stance could be if the leader previously coached a teacher, who returned with the same question or problem. The teacher may have

tried the solutions generated in the previous coaching conversation but is still experiencing the issue. Of course, the conversation that ensues will guide the leader to
the best approach, but consultation may be necessary for this situation. The critical
thing to remember is not to get stuck here too often. As leaders, be careful not to
make a practice of defaulting to consulting; if all leaders do is simply tell people how
to solve problems, it will be exhausting for the leader, and it will move them further
away from genuinely unlocking the human potential that exists within the staff.

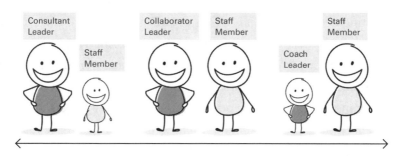

FIGURE 2.1: Three leadership stances.

There are situations when a leader must use an even more directive approach. This
is a form of consulting, but the conversation is more directive in nature. For example,
suppose a teacher has engaged in unacceptable behavior; the leader must give clear
feedback on what is unacceptable about the teacher's behavior and even more precise
feedback regarding what must change. Perhaps parents complain that the teacher
consistently raises her voice when struggling to get the students attention back after
group work. In fact, you may have witnessed this behavior yourself. The directive
might be "It is unacceptable for you to raise your voice with students. Please work
on using a consistent attention signal, practice the signal with students, and ensure
that you use a normal speaking voice in all interactions with students." In chapter 3
(page 55), we explore the responsibility to deal with conflict and challenges as a
leader and, for many of these situations, a direct approach will be necessary. You,
as a leader, will continuously be determining when the consultant stance or a more
direct approach is needed. It is good to remember, "*Coaching is not supervision, but
effective supervisors coach a lot*" (Bloom, Castagna, Moir, & Warren, 2005, p. 10).

Collaborator Stance

Leaders in this stance create a partnership with the teacher or staff member they
are working with. The leader is a co-learner and co-collaborator and often says, "Let's
think about this together," "How could we approach this situation?" or "What do we
need to consider before making a decision?" Figure 2.1 shows that both the leader
and the staff member are equal since they share their thinking and contributions to

problem solving. It is paramount that the leader engages the staff member in equally sharing ideas, or this could easily slip into a consultant stance. However, in some cases, leaders may make a conscious decision during the conversation to move into consulting to address a particular part of the problem or situation. It is plausible that a leader might shift stances throughout an interaction based on how the conversation evolves. For example, as a district leader, you meet with a principal who wants to problem solve a concern with a parent. You begin the conversation in collaboration, seeking to understand and asking questions for the principal to consider for resolving the issue. During the discussion, it becomes apparent the principal and some teachers have not been communicating with the parent and ignoring telephone calls, which has escalated the problem. You have tight expectations in your district that parents are well informed and communication is timely. You move into a more directive stance at this time to clarify your expectations. It is critically important that leaders remain present in the conversation and listen deeply throughout the interaction so they can suitably shift to the stance most in line with the individual's needs and most beneficial for the individual's continued growth and development.

Reflective Coaching Stance

Leaders may consider the coach stance when they feel staff members already have the answer within themselves. Leaders believe by asking the right questions, they can mediate the staff members' thinking, helping them recognize they already have the answer. This third stance aids staff in considering options and trusting their instincts. Reflective coaching conversations can contribute to the development of self-efficacy and self-direction that empowers and unlocks potential. Figure 2.1 (page 41) shows that in the coach stance, the staff member or teacher is contributing most to thinking and problem solving. In the reflective coach stance, the leader uses the pronouns *you* or *your* most, asking questions like, "In your experience, what is your first thought? Have you had a similar experience? How did you handle it?"

In the beginning of this chapter, we reference *unlocking potential* as the lens through which we would focus. We contend the reflective *coaching* stance is most likely to achieve this purpose but recognize that combining all three stances (consultant, collaborator, and coach) can accomplish this purpose. It is essential to reflect on your leadership style and understand the need to use all three stances from time to time. Relying on the one stance most comfortable for you as a leader and not venturing outside your comfort zone could lead to creating an unintentional reliance on you as the ultimate decision maker. This does not build human capacity or unlock potential. The next section will guide you through how to navigate and strategically pull together all three stances.

The Three Stances Together

In our experiences as leadership coaches, we find that occasionally it makes sense for principals and district staff to directly ask which stance they would like the leaders to take during the conversation. For instance, you might ask, "Do you want me to tell you how to handle the situation, collaborate with you to figure out the best option, or coach you through it?" Essentially, you are asking, "What stance would help you best right now?" If you always hear, "I just want you to consult," it is fine to start in that stance and shift stances when possible to mitigate the staff members' thinking and build their ability to be reflective toward self-improvement. It makes sense, at times, that staff will want a quick answer or they have already considered several ways to handle a situation and need another person's input. Asking the question, "What are some initial things you have thought about to solve the problem?" is an excellent way to get the conversation going, and demonstrates the positive presupposition that you believe the staff members have already thought about it. Sometimes, starting in one stance provides opportunities to move into other stances.

Let's consider the example from earlier in the Consultant Stance section of this chapter (see page 41). Sometimes a form of the consultant stance might include situations when a leader must use a more directive approach. Recall the teacher who consistently raised her voice with students when attempting to get their attention back after group work. The leader issued a directive that it is unacceptable for the teacher to raise her voice with students. The leader suggested the teacher use a consistent attention signal, practice the signal with students, and ensure a normal speaking voice in all interactions with students. The beauty here is the leader also created the possibility for collaborating and coaching through this directive. You can segue into collaboration by asking, "Would you like to think through different options for attention signals together?" Coaching can happen by asking the teacher what other options they have tried in the past or asking them to think about ways to elicit student attention without raising their voice. It would not have made sense to immediately ask reflective questions since you had a clear directive to communicate first. Moving into collaborating and coaching makes sense and supports the teacher as she works to improve the situation.

Figure 2.2. (page 44) provides descriptions of each stance and an opportunity for you to reflect as you determine which leadership stance to consider.

The next section offers questions to help leaders as they use the three stances in conversations with staff.

Considerations	Stance			Notes and Reflections
	Consultant	Collaborator	Reflective Coach	
How do I know which stance to choose?	• Need to build background knowledge (of new staff or a new position) or have limited knowledge about the topic. • Have policy or procedure questions. • Staff specifically ask for your advice. • A quick decision is necessary. • Need to communicate alignment with mission, vision, and values.	• Need to foster collaborative thinking as a way to consider options for problem solving. • The person has sufficient background knowledge and understanding of the factors contributing to the problem or issue. • Staff specifically ask you to help them think something through.	• Need to support the staff members' generation of ideas. • Need to foster staff reflection on practice. • Need to foster self-coaching and self-direction. • Staff specifically ask you to coach them through how to handle an issue or problem.	

What does the stance look and sound like?		
• Use a confident, credible voice. • Sit up straight to deliver the advice. • Use resources like policy manuals, and mission, vision, and values statements as tools to deliver the message. • Use the pronoun *I* (for example, I think it is essential to keep our values in mind when making this decision).	• Use a confident, credible voice. • Sit in a way that establishes a partnership (for example, side by side). • Reference shared resources strategically placed between the leader and the staff member. • Use the pronouns *we* and *you* and phrases like "Why don't we . . ." and "Let's think about . . ."	• Use an open, approachable voice. • Pay full attention to the staff member, and make strong eye contact. • Use the pronoun *you*, as in "So you are concerned about . . ." • When responding, use a pattern of pausing, paraphrasing, and inquiring to open thinking, or probe for specificity to focus thinking. • Frame invitational questions to support thinking, such as, "What might be some ways to . . . ?" "What are some options you are considering?" and "What are some of the connections you are making?"

Source for stances: Lipton & Wellman, 2003.

FIGURE 2.2: Using the three leadership stances.

*Visit **go.SolutionTree.com/PLCbooks** for a free reproducible version of this figure.*

Great Questions to Lead From Within

As mentioned previously, deep listening to understand is critical. Though it may not inherently seem this way, much of a leader's work revolves around conversations with teachers. At first, it can be tempting to dominate those conversations because leaders want to help and fix problems for people. Problem solving, in general, is a big part of being a leader. There is always a problem to solve. When your goal is for staff to self–problem solve and you recognize they may already have the answer, asking a few high-quality questions is an essential tool. This is a brave thing to do. The right question can be a catalyst for powerful reflection, problem solving, and ultimately, change. Learning to ask questions that will elicit self-exploration and unlock potential will help strengthen your practice as a leader and help set up others for success. Using questions demonstrates you are curious and want to know more about the situation, and that you, the leader, seek to understand the teacher's challenge, problem, or concern. Coaching thought leader Michael Bungay Stanier (2016), author of *The Coaching Habit: Say Less, Ask More and Change the Way You Lead Forever*, offers seven questions to guide leaders to help others generate their solutions without rushing to give them advice. Leaders often have what Stanier (2016) calls an "advice monster" living within that is itching to solve the problem for all who come to them with a concern (p. 2). Leaders must keep the advice monster at bay. Karen can genuinely relate to this. She is confident that anyone who worked in her school or district reading this would agree. Karen always had the advice monster with her as she led. She learned to lead more from within, and sought to understand, authentically listen, and guide conversations with questions; however, the advice monster always wanted to solve the problems first. As you consider your leadership style, reflect on Stanier's (2016) seven questions in figure 2.3 and how you can use them to guide your practice.

Stanier's (2016) Seven Questions	Notes and Reflections How can I build these into my leadership practice?
1. Kick-Start Question "What's on your mind?" This question gets you to what matters most quickly, so you can get to the real concern or issue.	

2. A.W.E. Question "And what else?" This is the best question because the first answer is never the only answer and often not the best answer. When you probe deeper for more answers and more possibilities, not only does it slow down the advice monster within, but it also generates possibilities and ideas the person may not have initially considered. This question also keeps the flames of curiosity burning bright!	
3. Focus Question "What's the real challenge here for you? The first two questions allow the leader to get to the heart of the matter. This question focuses directly on the person and how the issue directly affects them. The keywords in this question are *real* and *you*. Asking what the *real* challenge is and then asking *for you* provide the focus and clarity the leader needs to get to the next question, What do you want?	
4. Foundation Question "What do you want?" This question is often not easy for the person to answer, but it moves the conversation to a deeper level faster. It gets to the heart of what the person wants to happen related to the problem, concern, or issue, and keeps the conversation focused even when emotions are involved.	
5. Lazy Question "How can I help?" or "What do you want from me?" These questions work in two ways. First, they force the person to make an explicit request—to clarify what the person wants or needs help with. Second, they are self-management tools to keep you curious and lazy; these questions prevent you from spending time doing things *you think* the person wants you to do.	

FIGURE 2.3: The seven questions.

continued →

Stanier's (2016) Seven Questions	Notes and Reflections How can I build these into my leadership practice?
6. Strategic Question "If you say 'yes' to this, what must you say 'no' to?" If you're someone who feels compelled to say "yes" to every request or challenge, then this is the question for you. Overwhelmed and overcommitted, you've lost your focus and spread yourself too thin. This is why you must ask a strategic question; asking a "yes" without an attendant "no" is an empty promise. This question helps make the promise real.	
7. Learning Question "What was most useful or most valuable for you?" This question helps finish the conversation with a sense of accomplishment and meaning for both parties. Asking this question is an effortless way to reinforce learning and development. By asking people to identify and reflect on the process, this question helps create the space in which insightful moments of learning can occur. The question also assumes the conversation was helpful, providing a naturally meaningful conclusion to the discussion.	

Visit **go.SolutionTree.com/PLCbooks** *for a free reproducible version of this figure.*

In addition to Stanier's (2016) questions, we offer additional questions to enhance your leadership practices (Kintner-Duffy, 2017). Use figure 2.4 for additional reflection and as a tool to keep nearby as you consider situational leadership needs and how you can impact practice through asking questions.

Situation or Purpose	Potential Questions (Kintner-Duffy, 2017)	Notes How have I used these questions?
Elicit perspective.	How did it feel to . . . ? How comfortable are you . . . ? What means the most to you personally about this?	

Understand the issue, concern, problem, or focus.	What specifically are you hoping to achieve during our time together? What is your ultimate outcome from our discussion? Could you tell me more about why, how, or where . . . ?	
Make connections.	How is this behavior like . . . ? Could you describe a similar example of when you've encountered this obstacle? What conclusions can you draw about . . . ?	
Facilitate prediction.	What might happen if . . . ? What do you think the response would be if . . . ? What response or reaction are you most concerned about?	
Prompt thought processes.	What is your decision-making process at this moment? How do you know? What is your thinking about . . . ?	
Brainstorm.	How will you plan to . . . .? What are some ways you can . . . ? How will you include . . . ?	
Compare.	What do you think went well? What do you think did not go well? What was the difference between these moments?	

FIGURE 2.4: Situational questions.

Visit go.SolutionTree.com/PLCbooks for a free reproducible version of this figure.

Four Impactful Coaching Skills

To close this chapter, we want to leave you with four skills we both find very effective as we create space to listen and learn with others authentically. Too often, leaders struggle to stay focused on the conversation and problem at hand. It seems even more critical that leaders develop consistent habits to intentionally stay focused in today's constantly changing world. Whether you are using a consultant, collaborator, or reflective coach stance and all the great questions we suggest, you still must develop habits that provide focus and direction as you lead from within. We highly recommend you learn the skills of pausing, paraphrasing, positive presupposing, and probing from educators and coauthors Robert Garmston and Bruce Wellman (2016) to deepen more meaningful interactions.

Pausing

Pause three to five seconds before responding. By knowing you will pause, you can give your full attention to listening. The pause is your time to process what you heard. As you practice the art of pausing, the discussion slows, giving those in the conversation time to process the information and consider a response. In the classroom, teachers use pausing to provide students with precious wait time to dramatically improve their critical-thinking skills. Just as students need time to think before responding, so do leaders in coaching situations. Silence, even if initially uncomfortable, can be an excellent indicator of productive collaboration. The act of pausing creates a relaxed and yet purposeful atmosphere. Pausing also signals others' value; their ideas and comments are worth thinking about. Pausing dignifies people's contribution and implicitly encourages future participation. Pausing enhances discussion and dramatically increases the quality of decision making. Using a pause strategy as part of your coaching will increase your opportunity to remain in a coach stance. Consider when you might immediately practice pausing in a conversation to create space in the dialogue for intentional reflection.

Paraphrasing

As a listener, learn to *paraphrase* (or translate another's spoken or written words into your own words or to summarize) as part of your communication strategy. This strategy gives others confidence that you are listening and understand what is said. It also ensures you stay present in the conversation. Leaders often teach this strategy to collaborative teams. Paraphrasing can be built into the group's norms to ensure the team validates and considers all opinions when discussing student needs. For example, when data analysis for a root cause takes place, team norms could require teachers have comprehensive discussions, and through coaching, they can learn to pause and paraphrase as they listen to one another's thoughts. Understanding others will create synergy as the team collaborates to meet student needs. When you paraphrase as a leader, you connect with the other person on two levels: (1) content (*I understand your message*) and (2) emotion (*I care about you*).

Positive Presupposing

Leading from within requires a solid conviction to always assume others' intentions are positive. Your belief that others have good intentions and the desire and ability to learn and change are skills that help you build trust with those you lead. This presumes positive presupposing, and when practiced, it creates enhanced opportunities for coaching. Building on the skills of others and noticing their positive strengths, attitudes, and abilities, for example, create coachable moments. In our work with schools and districts, we have noticed the skill of positive presupposing takes an intentional mindset. From our experiences, it seems to require leaders to have great patience and courage to maintain a positive presupposition during difficult conversations and challenging situations. It seems people's natural tendencies often move out of a position of positive intent.

Probing

Probe for more information to fully understand the issue and the perspective of the person you are interacting with. This is extremely useful when emotions might be getting in the way of clear communication. For example, a staff member asks to speak to you about a concern. The person enters your office and immediately begins to dive into the conversation. It is clear the person is struggling to communicate the concern clearly and concretely, using phrases like "Everyone is upset about this" or "We have to change the way we do this because it is affecting so many students." Probing for more information will slow things down and help the person understand the concern and address the issue.

Challenges of a Coaching Approach

For leaders accustomed to tackling performance problems by telling people what to do, a coaching approach often feels too soft. What's more, it can make leaders psychologically uncomfortable because it deprives them of their most familiar management tool: asserting their authority. These leaders may resist coaching—and left to their own devices, they may not even give it a try. "I'm too busy," they'll say, or "This isn't the best use of my time," or "The people I work with aren't coachable." In psychologist Daniel Goleman's (2000) classic study of leadership styles, leaders ranked coaching as their least-favorite style, saying they simply didn't have time for the slow and tedious work of teaching people and helping them grow. In other words, using a coaching style of leadership often does not feel like they are accomplishing tasks and goals quickly, so many leaders will accept short-term quick fixes rather than building capacity within themselves and others. As a leader, taking on the challenge of developing skills, questioning techniques, and understanding which stance is needed will guide your practice and provide you with confidence as you empower others. Leading from within requires time and attention to the obstacles and challenges of leading others.

Wrap-Up

No matter your coaching experience, this is a skill set to incorporate into your leadership work. It involves intentionally being aware of the most impactful way to support others and using excellent communication skills to understand and develop the people you wish to lead. As you lead from within, you will spend more time identifying the needs of others and the approach that will be the most effective. As in the three stances, you may need to consult, collaborate, or practice reflective coaching. Create every opportunity to build your skill set to reflect and be thoughtful in your approach as a leader. In our opinion, this is not a soft skill or a leadership option. Learning to coach from within is necessary for leadership. Educators are in a people business, and the people whom they serve need leaders who can take the time to build relationships and support others through a coaching model. Practice and learn using the templates throughout this chapter and use the reflective tool at the end of this chapter to consider your next coaching steps. In chapter 3 (page 55), we examine strategies for dealing with conflict and challenges as you lead from within.

Six-Sentence Summary

The coaching approach to leadership provides an opportunity to be more in tune with the specific and individual motivations of those you lead. As a leader, you want to develop people who can problem solve and think through options, weighing the pros and cons of each. As leadership coaches, we aspire to coach more than tell and do our best to build capacity and potential whenever possible. We also know that there are times when we must guide and direct those we lead. As a leader, listen attentively and consider what you know about the speaker, and begin to understand the direction you want to take. Reflect and learn whether the person could benefit most from consulting, collaborating, or reflective coaching.

Making an Impact in Six: Leading With Coaching

The following six ideas provide opportunities for further reflection and action. We provide three reflections on what great leaders do and avoid doing to gain focus, as well as three considerations for how to make an impact in six minutes, six weeks, and six months to guide your leadership planning and practice.

Thoughtful Leaders Do . . .	Thoughtful Leaders Avoid . . .
1. Listen more and talk less.	Taking over conversations with their opinions
Current reality and next steps:	
2. Work on empowering their staff to be efficacious and self-aware.	Stepping in to solve problems for people
Current reality and next steps:	
3. Move through the leadership stances of consultant, collaborator, and reflective coach fluidly based on what they hear from the staff member they are working with.	Staying primarily in the leadership stance (consultant, collaborator, or reflective coach) they are most comfortable in
Current reality and next steps:	

4. What will you do in six minutes to lead like a coach?

For example:

Reflect on three conversations you had with staff throughout the day. Consider which stance you took during those conversations—consultant, collaborator, coach, or a combination of the stances. What parts of each conversation do you feel helped empower each individual? What can you celebrate? What might you do differently next time?

My ideas:

5. What will you do in six weeks to lead like a coach?

For example:

Use the reflective questions to guide conversations with staff (see page 46). Plan ahead of time what questions you might ask based on the nature of the conversation. After six weeks, identify the questions you use most. Consider your progress. Are there some questions that feel more comfortable than others? Are there some questions you want to try but have not used yet? What has been the response or reaction from those you have coached?

My ideas:

6. What will you do in six months to lead like a coach?

For example:

Each month, for six months, write down the overall celebrations and challenges you face as you work as a leader to build capacity and empower others. After six months, reflect on your progress and consider the next steps.

My ideas:

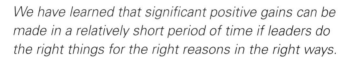

Chapter 3

Leading Through Conflict and Challenge

We have learned that significant positive gains can be made in a relatively short period of time if leaders do the right things for the right reasons in the right ways.

—Robert Eaker

Ocean Breeze Elementary School had a state-designated status of *F* when Mrs. Childress accepted the daunting task of leading the school as its principal. She had previously worked as an assistant principal in a school that had successfully engaged in school improvement using the PLC process. Relying on her previous knowledge and experience using the PLC process, she built a common understanding of the *why* and *what* of school-improvement work, providing leadership as the teachers developed collective commitments and established goals. Teachers worked in collaborative teams to identify student needs and received coaching and support from the school leadership team. Despite these efforts to build a solid foundation using the PLC process, Principal Childress faced many challenges along the way.

Early in the second term, Principal Childress called Karen asking for her guidance in understanding why she was seeing so much resistance to what she believed was the *right work* (the work that improves student learning). Why couldn't everyone see it this way? It made so much sense to her. Principal Childress and her leadership team were becoming very frustrated with several teachers who were constant naysayers. These teachers questioned every step in the school-improvement process and refused to do the work in some situations. As soon as Karen signed on to meet with the leadership team virtually, she saw the members' exhaustion and frustration. They shared these questions: Why were teachers still not all on board? What were they missing in understanding that this was the way to improve the school? Why did they not have the same sense of urgency Principal Childress and the leadership team had? The leadership team was disappointed that the teachers had not implemented many of its expectations. Could the teachers possibly be derailing the work intentionally? Or is this completely unintentional on the part of the teachers? As Karen talked with the team, she reminded members of her mantra, "Go slow to go fast," and that they would need to carefully sort out if the issue was a lack of understanding of how to implement the expectations or an unwillingness to comply.

As we explored in chapter 1 (page 9), being a brave leader requires strength to do whatever it takes to build capacity in others. Witnessing others not entirely on the same page as you tests the patience of every leader we have had the opportunity to work with. Unfortunately, leaders cannot ignore these situations; as a leader, you must listen and observe carefully to understand why some do not implement your tight expectations. Look in the mirror and ask, "What am I currently dealing with (or not dealing with), and how might those factors impact the school culture?" This careful consideration will inform your next steps.

In this chapter, we ask you to consider how you deal with difficult situations. Organizational experts Steve Gruenert and Todd Whitaker (2015) remind us, "The culture of any organization is shaped by the worst behavior the leader is willing to tolerate" (p. 36). Leaders can exacerbate situations and encourage harmful or destructive behaviors by simply not addressing them. Expectations in an organization are often more visible by what is "allowed" to happen than the officially stated *tights*—the leader's non-negotiable expectations. For example, as a principal, you may have a written norm that all teachers come to collaborative team meetings with their student data ready to share. You know one teacher consistently arrives unprepared. However, you have not addressed this because of this teacher's overall negative and difficult attitude. You find it exhausting to deal with her. You know the team will work around her, and you avoid the situation. You may not have considered the overall impact on the school culture that your lack of action is having. As you read this chapter, contemplate how you deal with (or choose not to deal with) complacency or a lack of adherence to expectations. To set your reflection for this chapter, pause and consider the following guiding questions.

- What leadership strategies do you use when faced with conflict in your organization?

- Do you confront the elephant in the room, or do you accept noncompliant behaviors because it makes you feel uncomfortable to deal with conflict?

- Are you looking at behaviors to understand what motivates those behaviors, or are the behaviors simply frustrating you?

- What are the hidden messages in your actions?

- How are you managing the change process?

- What can you do differently to ensure everyone in your system focuses on the right work even when they do not believe in the purpose or have the same sense of commitment to student growth as you?

Use figure 3.1 to reflect on these questions and set your intentions. As you note and document your responses, consider how this chapter can help build your leadership skills.

Guiding Question	Personal Reflection	What will help me improve and take next steps?
What are you currently dealing with (or not dealing with) that is impacting your school culture?		
What leadership strategies do you use when you are faced with conflict in your organization?		
Do you confront the elephant in the room, or do you accept noncompliant behaviors because it makes you feel uncomfortable to deal with conflict?		
Are you looking at behaviors to understand what is motivating those behaviors, or are the behaviors simply frustrating you?		
Contemplate how you deal with (or choose not to deal with) complacency. What hidden messages are in your actions?		

FIGURE 3.1: Guiding questions for reflection as you lead through conflict and challenge.

continued →

Guiding Question	Personal Reflection	What will help me improve and take next steps?
How are you managing the change process?		
What can you do differently to ensure everyone in your system focuses on the right work even when they do not believe in the purpose or have the same sense of commitment to student growth as you?		

*Visit **go.SolutionTree.com/PLCbooks** for a free reproducible version of this figure.*

A Sense of Urgency

Principal Childress discovered what PLC experts Richard DuFour, Rebecca DuFour, Robert Eaker, Thomas W. Many, and Mike Mattos (2016) explain:

> A staff that have built a solid foundation for a PLC by carefully crafting consensus regarding their purpose, the school they seek to create, their collective commitments, the specific goals they will use to monitor their progress, and the strategies for achieving those goals *have not eliminated the possibility of conflict.* (p. 212, italics added)

School improvement is a continuous process. Immediate actions can have impact, but long-term sustainable change takes time. Creating systems and processes is essential, but they do not replace the need to constantly build shared understanding and address staff members' challenges and conflicting behaviors and views. In an ideal world, a principal could flip a switch and all staff would believe in the work necessary to improve their school. You would announce a change, and the light would come on. All teachers would urgently understand and implement the change. However, instead of an on-off light switch, change often works more like a dimmer switch. As you dial the dimmer switch to the right, the room slowly moves from dark to light in increments, because the brutal reality is that change is hard, and people must keep taking baby steps toward change. Leaders of large and small organizations are challenged daily to implement change and ask others to follow. Experts have written and revised change-management theories for years. For example, professor, author, and founder of a management consulting firm John P. Kotter's (2008, 2012) eight-step process to change theory begins with urgency.

1. Establish a sense of urgency.

2. Create a guiding coalition.

3. Develop a vision and strategy.

4. Communicate the change vision.

5. Empower employees for broad-based action.

6. Generate short-term wins.

7. Consolidate gains and produce more change.

8. Anchor new approaches in the culture.

Despite the wide adoption of his change theory, schools and organizations often fail at implementing change. The model assumes urgency; in other words, everyone in the organization will change their behaviors because leaders have a sense of urgency. Kotter (2008) felt so strongly about the need to establish urgency he states in *A Sense of Urgency*, "At the very beginning of any effort to make changes of any magnitude, if a sense of urgency is not high enough and complacency is not low enough, everything else becomes so much more difficult" (p. ix). Kotter (2008) continues that *complacency* works opposite of *urgency*, and "it is much more common than we might think and very often invisible to the people involved" (p. ix). Principal Childress, the elementary school principal from the beginning of this chapter, recognized complacency early in the change process, and is working to address behaviors demonstrating the preference to accept the status quo of being an *F* school rather than doing the hard work to make successful changes. Principal Childress also understood that her teachers may be unintentionally complacent; she knows not everyone has the same sense of urgency she and her leadership team have. This realization is a significant step in understanding how to address the conflict and challenges you face every day.

In his book, *Upstream*, author Dan Heath (2020) cites countless examples of leaders who are willing to prevent a problem systematically before it happens (*upstream thinking*), rather than having to reduce the harm those problems cause (*downstream thinking*). If you are swimming upstream, you are moving closer to where the trouble started or getting to the root cause. People teach a child to swim rather than doing a rescue, and in the case of school leadership, effective leaders work to prevent problems instead of waiting to react to the fallout. One effective upstream thinking process common in successful schools is response to intervention (RTI).

With this focus, teachers and leaders identify and address each student's needs and the root causes for a lack of learning. Implementation of three tiers of intervention allows for differentiated instruction and immediate and timely response to meet the needs of students. As Heath (2020) describes, with upstream thinking, leaders focus on prevention. Tier 1 of the RTI process provides an opportunity for teachers and leaders to focus on effective core instruction which prevents the need for many students to need further interventions as part of Tiers 1 and 2. Addressing the learning gaps at Tier 2 and Tier 3 is necessary, but when they are the only focus in a school and first-best instruction is ignored, it is an example of downstream leadership. As leaders build the PLC and RTI processes in schools, teachers have an opportunity to apply upstream thinking using collaboration and a focus on learning and results to meet the needs of students, instead of being isolated and overwhelmed (downstream thinking). Heath (2020) also says downstream situations often lead back to an upstream solution. Leaders can learn from mistakes or inaction and see what practices and solutions they need to implement as prevention. Leading from within requires a more intentional mindset on prevention and creating a sense of urgency focused on the root cause of a problem.

Reflection

Think about a time when you tried to implement a change. What roadblocks were in your way? How did you handle them? What were your successes and challenges? What sense of urgency did you create? Was your thinking preventive (upstream) or more reactive (downstream)?

Behavior Before Belief

Researcher, speaker, and author Douglas Reeves (2020) states the blunt reality of change:

> If people will not change when the alternative is dying a painful death and missing experiences with those they love, then why would anyone expect that creating a sense of urgency for educational systems, corporations, or nonprofit organizations is going to lead to change? There is prevailing mythology of change leadership: if we just find the right blend of persuasion, research, and emotional appeal, then staff will embrace the changes leaders wish to make. This false belief is based on the myth of *buy-in*—that is, to implement effective change, leaders must first gain widespread staff agreement. When leaders tell

me they have buy-in from all staff members, one of two things is true:
(1) they are not really asking for significant changes or, more likely,
(2) the real resistance is happening underground, out of the leader's
earshot. This is why the vast majority of change initiatives fail. (p. 104)

The frustration of Principal Childress's leadership team is a good sign it knows it is asking for significant changes and the resistance to change is apparent. The team also recognizes it must confront the obstacles impeding implementation. How do team members work differently? What will it take to see behaviors change? How do principals change the conversations so they are leading from the premise that behavior precedes belief? In chapter 2 (page 37), we shared insights into the many benefits of the coaching process. Learning opportunities exist that allow for thinking and shared decision making through coaching conversations and questions. Leaders can guide a mindset shift rather than insisting on it.

We have both learned (sometimes the challenging way!) it is not just that we lead and others simply follow. In our early days as leaders, we are confident we erroneously led through this distorted way of thinking. We assumed the power of our word, the urgency in our voice, and modeling of what we expected would be enough to sway even the deepest nonbelievers. Karen, for example, distinctly remembers a time when she was urgently trying to implement the PLC process as a superintendent in all of her district's thirty-eight schools. She held professional development sessions and developed tight expectations, knowing it was exemplary work for her schools. For the most part, her principals understood the need for school improvement and were doing their very best to lead the changes needed in their schools. All seemed to be going well until the teacher's union executive asked to meet with Karen. The union executive explained that if she didn't slow down, teachers would organize serious resistance to the changes. The union executive did Karen a great favor by expressing the teachers' feelings. Teachers were overwhelmed, and even though they understood the necessary work, it was too much at once. Karen met with the principals, and they collectively breathed a sigh of relief. Karen didn't know how much conflict and resistance the principals were dealing with in their schools, and it was indeed time to take a few steps back to let the implementation processes deepen—one step at a time. Karen worked with the principals to consider the first necessary practices to put in place. By doing this, time was available to deepen understanding as the teachers moved toward behavior before belief.

Fortunately, we continue to learn it takes much more than influence to change, and a great place to start is to insist on expected practices. When you lead from within, you seek to understand your own *why*; in other words, your purpose (mission) and the vision of what you wish your school or district to become. Visualize where you will be in one year as a system and work toward that vision with unflinching intention. Once internalized, you can focus on the tights or the behavior expectations for how the staff will work together. For instance:

> *We will work as a school, exemplifying the effective research-based practices evident in successful schools. We will have expectations for our students as if they are all capable of achieving rigorous, grade-level learning. We will collaborate as if all our expertise will be needed to address our students' concerns. We will deal with facts and evidence as if this is how we always have functioned. We will manage conflict effectively as if we have always been open to learning from one another as we build successful practices in the service of students. This is how we will behave because it is the proper work to do. These will be our tights—our non-negotiable behaviors.*

Use figure 3.2 to consider the previous examples of *behavior before belief* actions. Note how you can implement similar measures, and add your suggestions to the list.

Behavior Before Belief Action (As if . . .)	What is the current evidence that staff practice behavio before belief in my school or district?	What are the next steps I can take to improve on this practice?
We work *as if* we are an *A school*, exemplifying the effective research-based practices evident in successful schools.	Example: We are implementing the PLC process with fidelity and have tight expectations, and all teachers collaborate in teams to address the four PLC questions: (1) What do we want students to know and be able to do?, (2) How do we know when they have learned it?, (3) What do we do when they haven't learned it?, and (4) How do we extend learning for those who have learned it? (DuFour et al., 2016). Your practice:	Example: We are deepening our practice of using common formative assessment data to inform interventions and extensions, and expect all teams to provide Tier 2 interventions. We offer professional learning with coaching follow-up to all teachers to support and deepen this work. Your next steps:

We have expectations for students *as if* they are all capable of achieving rigorous, grade-level learning.	Example: Teachers work from grade-level standards, writing student learning targets and aligning assessments and instruction to the rigor of these standards. Teachers expect all students to master these grade-level standards. Teachers understand some students need more time and support. Your practice:	Example: We provide ongoing professional development on differentiating instruction, so Tier 1 interventions and extensions are more effective. Your next steps:
We collaborate *as if* all our expertise is needed to address students' concerns.	Example: We collectively establish scoring criteria and score student work together to calibrate our expectations. We examine the student results together to address the needs of all students in our grade level or content area. Your practice:	Example: We continue to learn more about identifying the root cause and expect all collaborative teams to dig deeply to understand *why* a student cannot read or do mathematics. The next steps for Tier 2 interventions and extensions continue to grow from these data. Your next steps:

FIGURE 3.2: Reflection—behavior before belief.   continued ➔

Behavior Before Belief Action (As if . . .)	What is the current evidence that staff practice behavior before belief in my school or district?	What are the next steps I can take to improve on this practice?
We deal with facts and evidence *as if* this is how we always have functioned.	Example: Collaborative teams are expected to continuously look at and use data to inform their instructional next steps. Classroom observations provide feedback on what teams determine as next steps based on data. Your practice:	Example: We hold data talks with each collaborative team and the administrative team monthly. We expect teams to provide evidence of their data use to inform the next steps for each student. Your next steps:
We manage conflict effectively *as if* we have always been open to learning from one another as we build successful practices in the service of students.	Example: Each team reviews norms at the beginning of its collaborative team meeting. One person on the team is responsible for bringing attention to noncompliance of norms when necessary. Your practice:	Example: We continue to revisit and review our collective commitments as we hold one another accountable for the non-negotiable expectations in our school. These collective commitments continue to impact the norms of each collaborative team. Your practice:

*Visit **go.SolutionTree.com/PLCbooks** for a free reproducible version of this figure.*

Relationship Conflict Versus Task Conflict

Walking into a school for the first time as coaches, we are greeted by a young principal eager for support and frustrated beyond belief. Before we have our coats off, we learn there is significant conflict on the collaborative teams, and the principal is genuinely unsure how to handle all the disagreements. He describes a collaborative team engaging in very hostile conversations. Teachers appear to be struggling to like one another, let alone work together. The young principal often overhears sarcasm and negative comments that are hurtful to others. On another team, the conflicts appear to be more about the work. The team members disagree on scoring guides for their assessments, resulting in extremely long, frustrating conversations. The teachers debate student proficiency and struggle to agree on the level of rigor they should use to instruct and assess student work. This young principal is looking for a solution that will resolve both scenarios.

Author Adam Grant (2021) in *Think Again* shares excellent insight into these two very different types of conflict. He references Australian organizational psychologist Karen "Etty" Jehn, who uses the terms "relationship conflict" and "task conflict" (as cited in Grant, 2021, p. 78). In the young principal's school, the first collaborative team is most definitely suffering from relationship conflict, and the second team is deeply involved in task conflict. Using Jehn's definitions of conflict, Grant (2021) surveyed hundreds of new teams in Silicon Valley (California) during their first six months working together. When they finished their surveys, Grant (2021) asked managers to evaluate each team's effectiveness:

> The teams that performed poorly started with more relationship conflict than task conflict. They entered into personal feuds early on and were so busy disliking one another that they didn't feel comfortable challenging one another. It took months for many of the teams to make real headway on their relationship issues, and by the time that they did manage to debate key decisions, it was often too late to rethink their directions. (p. 78)

On the other hand, Grant (2021) reports the teams that started with task conflict found a way to resolve differences of opinion and move in a direction that allowed them to come together to produce what they needed. They spent less time in conflict and more time in problem solving.

We believe Grant's (2021) work supports our view that *relationship conflict* is detrimental to team performance; it will stand in the way of the vital work of reviewing, revising, and rethinking, while *task conflict* often provides a stronger sense of collaboration and outcome. In the young principal's school, he needed to be concerned and deal with the issues of the first team. The second collaborative team would still require monitoring and support; however, its members would likely learn to work together more effectively as their collaboration around shared goals increased. Task conflict encourages rethinking, challenges the status quo, and often pushes teams to produce more quality work. The young principal would do well to promote professional task conflict and create opportunities for constructive feedback. Of course, he must still manage this to ensure the loudest voices are not the only ones heard on the team. One way to build more vital collaboration is to use protocols as the structure to provide an opportunity for all team members to weigh in on the work. Addressing team norms is also critical to ensure respectful discourse. It's crucial that the young principal monitor the discourse, ensuring it stays focused on process (*how*) and not *why*. As Grant (2021) states, "When we argue about why, we run the risk of becoming emotionally attached to our positions and dismissive of the other side's" (p. 92). We believe the principal should monitor conversations to ensure the focus remains on *what* and *how*, not on an emotional defense of a position.

Considering the first collaborative team with relationship conflict, we asked the young principal to observe the team members' personalities. Were patterns of behaviors identifiable and, more importantly, characteristic of one or two team members? Was one (or more) teacher leading the dysfunction? We also asked him to consider what he had already attempted to do in dealing with this situation. Understanding the behaviors driving the conversations will help this young principal address the challenges of the team. Most importantly, if the behaviors continue, they can negatively impact the entire school culture. Toxic school cultures are bred and often grow from tiny seeds of conflict. School and district leaders must be attuned to these and take the necessary steps to create opportunities for positive change. Let's now look at ways to identify toxic behaviors within a conflict.

Toxic Behaviors

As Principal Childress continued to improve her school culture, she recognized the value of understanding her people. She had a few teachers who were intentionally or unintentionally creating roadblocks to deep implementation. Principal Childress knew it was critically important for her to ensure the behaviors of the adults in her school were representative of the school's mission and vision. During a coaching session, Karen asked her to consider her staff using four categories school culture expert and author Anthony Muhammad (2018) writes about in his best-selling book, *Transforming School Culture*. Muhammad (2018) says four unique groups each impact school culture. Two of the groups actively try to work against the school's priorities and belief systems. One is in the center of the disagreements and disruptions (*fundamentalists*), and another is just trying to get through each day (*survivors*). Muhammad (2018) writes, "in order to transform from a toxic to a healthy learning environment, it is essential for leaders to understand and influence change within these groups" (p. 39). In other words, deal with behaviors not positively impacting the culture of the school. Principal Childress applied this thinking to her staff, and in doing so, she recognized that she did have a few teachers who were intentionally working against the school's priorities. In our coaching roles, we often use Muhammad's (2018) descriptions to aid leaders in reflecting and considering their next steps. The following four paragraphs supply examples of how each of Muhammad's four descriptions present themselves in schools.

The young principal discussed earlier discovered that the team with relationship conflict was the result of one *fundamentalist* who truly did not want change (or to do the work necessary to improve the school), and was resentful of a hardworking teacher with a very positive mindset (who allowed herself to be drawn into the conflict). The principal needed to address the fundamentalist behavior to get this team on track. Do you have any staff who are intentionally causing a toxic culture by purposefully working against your expectations? We consider this group (fundamentalists) the most challenging when expecting and implementing behavioral changes. Their lack of trust in leaders and the mission and vision of the school or district complicates a leader's ability to influence behaviors. You cannot just wait for this group's belief in the changes to take hold; tight expectations are vital at the same time you are building a shared understanding of the purpose and, hopefully, adding to the trust and respect team members have for you as a leader. Many of the schools we work with have low student performance and perhaps have had many leadership changes over the years. Often, past leaders implemented several strategies to improve the school, and unfortunately, the fundamentalists who demonstrate a "this too shall pass" attitude may influence the staff. Some fundamentalists believe if they provide enough resistance and cause enough unpleasantness for leaders, the leaders may leave or stop expecting the work to change. It takes much courage to accept that you must have difficult conversations and confront the current reality to change this culture.

Can you identify any staff who are only *surviving*, which prevents them from taking more initiative and implementing expectations to the level needed to improve (*survivors*)? What support and coaching will they need to move from surviving to believing? Is it will or skill? In our experience, leaders often overlook their impact by providing more coaching and support to the survivors. They can fall under the radar as leaders see noticeable disruptions or negativity from fundamentalists who truly stand in the way of progress. Still, leaders fail to recognize that if they have struggling staff, these staff members can also prevent improvement.

Muhammad's third category, *believers*, is the teachers who have high expectations and belief in each student's ability to be successful. They have a student-centered mindset and do everything in their power to have ideal learning conditions for students. Obviously, this group of educators provides a positive influence for school improvement.

Finally, Muhammad's fourth descriptor is of the *tweeners*—teachers new to the profession or perhaps new to the school community. The fundamental need of tweeners is to find stability within the organization and understand how they can contribute to the overall goals. This final group does not resist the change process.

Use figure 3.3 to reflect on Muhammad's four descriptions and the behaviors of adults in your organization, and then create action steps to address any toxic behaviors getting in the way of school or district improvement.

Overall Driver of Behaviors (Muhammad, 2018)	Behavior Group Who are your believers, tweeners, survivors, and fundamentalists?	Concerns and Next Steps
Academic success for each student *Believers* have high expectations for students and are all in. They exhibit high levels of intrinsic motivation and have a willingness to confront opposing viewpoints. They are often teachers with at least three years of experience and varied pedagogical skills. This group is one of two that have the most impact on school improvement.		

Organizational stability These are the new or new-to-the organization teachers (or *tweeners*) who do not have tight bonds with the school or community—yet. They are often very enthusiastic about their new roles; however, they are cautious and may operate out of compliance for fear of losing their jobs. They need to have relationships with colleagues and leaders who show interest in their lives to build a trusting bond that will keep them and grow them in the profession.		
Emotional and mental survival These teachers have entirely given up on improving their practice and are focusing all their energy on just surviving the school year (*survivors*). Typically, they include a small group of educators (about 2 percent) of the staff. If left alone, this small group of educators can have a devastating impact on student success.		
Maintaining the status quo These are experienced educators who believe the traditional model of schooling is the only way to practice (*fundamentalists*). They are relentless in their attempts to discourage change and protect the existing system. *Change* is the enemy, and anyone who challenges the system is a threat to them. This is the other group with the most influence, and leaders must understand and address these behaviors if they wish to improve their school culture.		

FIGURE 3.3: Reflection—adult behaviors.

*Visit **go.SolutionTree.com/PLCbooks** for a free reproducible version of this figure.*

Honest and Respectful Conversations

Ideally, all leaders are comfortable having frank conversations with others and make this part of their daily practice, as needed. However, we find in our leadership coaching work this is not the case. Honest conversations are often challenging for many leaders. Despite knowing behaviors and attitudes can interfere with needed changes in the school or district, it is difficult to know the right time and the right way to have these conversations. For example, Principal Childress was unsure if the situations she described to Karen were severe enough to warrant critical discussions or if more time would give teachers the space to accept the needed changes and move forward. What is the best way to approach a fundamentalist? Will there be more negative backlash if Principal Childress deals with this now rather than wait and see if the situation improves? In our coaching work, we often find that the conversation is long overdue by the time a leader seeks advice. Recognizing if you are avoiding these conversations as a leader is an essential step in increasing your impact.

Reflection

Do you have any adult behavior concerns you need to address? What are your next steps?

As stated earlier, communicating your tight behavior expectations that are "just the way we work here" before you see beliefs change is always helpful when dealing with resistance. The school or district priorities are a valuable resource. Aligning what you expect to the stated values provides a critical link, setting the stage for conversations that insist staff live the espoused values. Like the top section of an iceberg, *espoused values* are the part of the culture people see. These values live above the waterline, where they are mission statements, values documents, and so on. What happens below the waterline—where the more significant part of the iceberg lives—is what matters. Do your staff's behaviors below the waterline match the espoused values and beliefs that live above the waterline? For example, in Principal Childress's district, expectations are built on four values: (1) quality instructional leadership, (2) quality first-time instruction, (3) effective social-emotional learning, and (4) effective classroom management. These are the curriculum and instructional priorities. As principal, she has these tools as she considers conversations with resisters. As Karen talked further with Principal Childress, it was clear the expected tight behaviors were well communicated and modeled at her school. Many teachers felt the leadership team's urgency to improve the school and upheld the non-negotiable expectations. Principal Childress could identify the few teachers negatively influencing others and causing resistance to change. She could see the behaviors from figure 3.3 (page 68), and thankfully, she was ready to have respectful, meaningful conversations with each type. Principal Childress understood she should be well prepared for these discussions and adapted some of the following suggestions from coauthors Kerry Patterson, Joseph Grenny, Ron McMillan, and Al Switzler (2012) for engaging in honest and respectful dialogue to address conflict.

1. Clarify what you want and what you do not want from the conversation—for yourself and the other person—before initiating and creating a safe environment for the discussion.

2. Clarify if you will address a specific incident of behavior, a pattern of repeated conduct, or the impact of the behavior on the individual's relationship with others.

3. Be concise when you present the problem, using facts rather than opinions.

4. Attempt to find mutual purpose by encouraging the individual to share his or her facts and opinions.

5. Explain both the natural consequences and the potential for disciplinary action if the behavior continues and what specific behaviors you expect.

Considering these five steps, it is essential to notice the overall theme of the conversation is factual; stick to the facts and identify the gaps between behavior and expectations. Of great value is your ability as a leader to organize your thoughts around the facts, behaviors, expectations, and any follow-through needed. Of course, staying calm and rational helps; however, you want to deliver a strong message with confidence and respect.

When entering into a difficult conversation, it can be helpful to consider using what nonverbal communications expert Michael Grinder calls a "third point" (as cited in Broom, 2021). Grinder refers to *two-point communication* as two people talking to each other, and *three-point communication* as two people talking to each other plus a third entity like a piece of paper, PowerPoint, and so on (as cited in Broom, 2021). When the interaction is not contentious, two-point communication is the best way to proceed. When the exchange is contentious, three-point communication may be the best route. Here's how it works. When it begins to feel unsettling during an interaction, you shift the focus of attention to the third entity. In the previous example, Principal Childress may decide to use the four expectations as the focal point of her conversations with resisters. She could simply lay the four-expectations document on the table and use it as the third entity. This transfers the attention of both parties to the document, lessening the stress by separating the content from the relationship.

Use figure 3.4, with suggestions from Patterson and colleagues (2012), to reflect on a necessary conversation you should have to address a current conflict. How can these five steps assist you with this critical work?

Step in the Critical Conversation Process (Patterson et al., 2012)	Your Reflections on How This Can Be Successful What will you do to prepare and consider?	Next Steps and Reflections After the Conversation What worked and what didn't work?
1. Clarify what you want and what you do not want from the conversation—for yourself and the other person—before initiating and creating a safe environment for the discussion. Example: Ms. Jay refuses to bring student data to her collaborative team meeting. The team leader has attempted to address this behavior, but it continues to disrupt the work of the team. You suspect Ms. Jay is resisting the collaborative work intentionally. You preplan for the meeting by writing down the action you wish to address and your expected outcome (that is, Ms. Jay comes prepared to share her student data at all team meetings, as required). You know Ms. Jay finds you and your office intimidating, so you ask to meet her in her classroom during her planning time.		
2. Clarify if you will address a specific incident of behavior, a pattern of repeated conduct, or the impact of the behavior on the individual's relationship with others. Example follow-through: Your email to Ms. Jay states you will meet her on Tuesday at 2:00 p.m. in her classroom to discuss the expectation of preparing and sharing student data at collaborative team meetings.		

3. Be concise when you present the problem, using facts rather than opinions. Example: The meeting begins with you giving Ms. Jay clarity on the tight expectation that all teachers come prepared to discuss student data with their collaborative team. You provide an example of another collaborative team's data set, and show Ms. Jay how the team uses the data to support all students.		
4. Attempt to find mutual purpose by encouraging the individual to share his or her facts and opinions. Example: Ms. Jay has an opportunity to express her opinion, and she shares that she is nervous about having other teachers see how poorly her students are doing. You ask Ms. Jay what you can do to help her. You explain that collectively, the teachers will be able to help her meet the needs of her students, and they can all share instructional expertise. This is impossible if they do not see her data and student work. You ask her to provide you with those data before the meeting and offer to go over them with her. She agrees.		
5. Explain both the natural consequences and the potential for disciplinary action if the behavior continues and what specific behaviors you expect. Example: You remind Ms. Jay of the expectation that she will begin to collaborate with her team using her student data. If her behavior doesn't change, you will indicate it in her personnel file. Again, you asked for her data set before the next collaborative team meeting to review it and support her. You expect her to participate at the team meeting, and you will follow up with her after a meeting to determine how productive this process was and what next steps are necessary.		

FIGURE 3.4: Steps in critical conversations.

*Visit **go.SolutionTree.com/PLCbooks** for a free reproducible version of this figure.*

Consensus on Collective Commitments

In the coaching conversation with Principal Childress's leadership team, Karen noticed the team assumed it had built a common understanding of the needed changes with everyone, so perhaps it was unnecessary to revisit. They had developed a mission and vision and believed teachers should know the expectations. As previously stated, this is not uncommon for leaders and leadership teams to assume. When you have created a sense of urgency, and staff seem to deeply understand the changes needed, it seems reasonable to expect the required behaviors will follow. Unfortunately, if it were this easy, we wouldn't be writing this chapter.

One next step Principal Childress and her team agreed to take was to ask teachers to write and agree on collective commitments to the vision and mission. In other words, although the mission defines their purpose and the vision statement explains what they want to become, Principal Childress and her team had not spent any time asking teachers to consider what behaviors the mission and vision require of the adults in the school. Karen asked the team to lead an exercise with the staff, providing time and space for teachers to contribute to the collective commitments (values) to accomplish the vision and mission. The goal of the activity is to come to a consensus on a short list of collective commitments. Consider why *consensus* is a critical step in this process. Why is it necessary for Principal Childress and her team to take the time to build consensus? We agree that the easiest way to have collective commitments might be to write them as a leadership team and give them to the staff. We also agree this will *not* lead to the changes you wish to see. It is important to remember you cannot wait for all staff to believe in the collective commitment statements and treat them as tights. This is why having consensus (versus 100 percent commitment) on expected behaviors will give you support to move forward. As DuFour and colleagues (2016) state, "If . . . the members of the organization have specified collective commitments, leaders operate with the full weight of the moral authority of the group behind them" (p. 41).

Principal Childress's leadership team agreed to use the following process to develop collective commitments. The members set aside two hours of a professional development day to begin this work, and they intentionally divided their teachers into groups of three. They used breakout rooms to structure the conversations, and followed these steps.

1. Discuss why collective commitments are an essential next step. (Fifteen minutes)

2. Revisit mission and vision statements. In the small groups of three, teachers review the mission and vision statements together and unpack them to understand. (Ten minutes)

3. Write collective commitments. Each small group writes ten collective commitments they are willing to honor as behaviors and that align with the vision and mission. Use the sentence starter, *We will* . . . (Thirty minutes)

4. Have teachers rejoin the larger group, and ask each small group to share its ten commitments on a shared poster or screen. Use a carousel activity, so each group has the opportunity to visit other groups. (Twenty minutes)

5. Begin creating consensus by putting all the groups' commitments into one slide presentation. Give each group all the slides and ask members to review all collective commitments to determine a total of five to eight they feel are the most important. If teachers can move from a poster or table around the room, you can do a *dot consensus*, where each group places colored dots on charts (other than their own) to mark which commitments seem to be the most important to them. (Thirty minutes)

6. The larger group reconvenes, and each small group submits its list of five to eight most-important collective commitments. The leadership team explains it will review the lists for overlap and draft *collective commitments* for the teacher groups to study again.

7. Continue to build consensus by reconvening the small groups of teachers at a follow-up staff meeting, giving each group a draft of the collective commitments. The groups consider the draft and use this question to guide the conversation: Are there any commitments on the draft that you cannot live with?

8. Reconvene the larger group to find consensus. Have each small group state whether it is ready to agree on the list (for example, using fist to five). If a majority is ready and accepting, you can now move to the final step. If you do not have a consensus, you will need more time in small groups to continue the work.

9.   To confirm each individual's agreement, ask each teacher to meet with the principal to sign off on the collective commitments.

Principal Childress and her staff's hard work produced the following collective commitments.

We will:

- Create and analyze data from common formative and summative assessments, and administer them according to the team's agreed-on timeline

- Commit to growing professionally as an individual and team

- Engage in open and frequent two-way communication with all stakeholders

- Commit to making all decisions in the best interest of students

- Come to work each day as the best version of ourselves, ready to share responsibilities and consider all points of view

- Show good customer service to students, staff, community members, and parents

- Work together to ensure all staff members use best practices that support student learning at the highest levels

- Model, encourage, and plan for student and staff celebrations as part of our culture

- Honor the individual and unique qualities of our students and staff, and not use their uniqueness to label them

Wrap-Up

We often say that district and school leaders should have human resource training as part of their certification. In other words, much of the work of educational leadership involves developing relationships and understanding the adults in the system. Leaders know students must be the priority in a school, so leaders work from within to address the conflicts and challenges that arise with the adults in the system so they do not negatively impact students. Use the reflective tool at the end of this chapter (page 78) to consider your next coaching steps. In chapter 4 (page 81), we examine strategies for leading change with accountability.

Six-Sentence Summary

Leading from within tests the patience of every leader we have had the pleasure to work with. Leaders can exacerbate situations and encourage harmful or destructive behaviors by simply not addressing them. Expectations in an organization are often more visible by what the leader "allows" to happen than the officially stated *tights*—the leader's non-negotiable expectations. In theory, leaders would lead, and everyone would follow. It takes much more than influence to change, and a great place to start is to insist on the practice of what the leader expects. Leaders build a consensus of collective commitments by acknowledging the need to develop a collective understanding of the right work.

Making an Impact in Six: Leading Through Conflict and Challenge

The following six ideas provide opportunities for further reflection and action. We provide three reflections on what great leaders do and avoid doing to gain focus, as well as three considerations for how to make an impact in six minutes, six weeks, and six months to guide your leadership planning and practice.

Thoughtful Leaders Do . . .	Thoughtful Leaders Avoid . . .
1. Recognize that a sense of urgency is essential but not easily transferred to others, and that complacency exists and is a barrier to change.	Assuming if they feel a sense of urgency to create change, there is no complacency in the organization and others will naturally follow their lead
Current reality and next steps:	
2. Create tight expectations for behaviors. For example, *We will behave as if we believe all students can learn at high levels, even before all staff believe in the success of these practices.*	Waiting for all staff to come on board before expecting behaviors to change and implementing successful school-improvement practices in the system
Current reality and next steps:	
3. Identify and address behavior characteristics causing an unhealthy culture and resistance to change.	Acknowledging that it is necessary to address toxic behaviors and take action to create change
Current reality and next steps:	

4. What will you do in six minutes to lead through conflict and challenge?

For example:

- Have an honest, respectful conversation with one person on your staff who is struggling to implement practice before belief. Look for every opportunity to build a shared understanding of the *why* of the work; however, intentionally confirm the need for alignment between everyday actions and non-negotiable expectations.

- Observe a collaborative team meeting with the intended purpose of learning the team's norms and how members work together. Celebrate their successful practices and guide them back to their norms if necessary.

My ideas:

5. What will you do in six weeks to lead through conflict and challenge?

For example:

- Use the steps to lead a collective commitment exercise with your staff (see page 74). Collect the drafts from each group. Build consensus on the most common suggested commitments and revisit this together as a staff in a few weeks. Repeat the exercise using the shared commitments and move forward with a list of agreed-on collective commitments for the entire staff. Ask all collaborative teams to build their team norms based on the collective commitments. Attend team meetings with an intentional focus on seeing the collective commitments come to life through the teams' norms.

- Plan leadership team or guiding coalition meeting agendas focusing on building shared understanding of the importance of consensus building as a staff and on each collaborative team. Model for this leadership team how it can facilitate each collaborative team meeting to build a culture of consensus around the needs of students. With the leadership team, explore the need to ensure practice before belief and aid members in understanding that to lead from within, all staff must commit to the tight expectations you have set for the school. Observe collaborative team meetings as a follow-up to support and ensure lead teachers understand how to build consensus and lead discussions that foster collective commitments to tight expectations.

My ideas:

6. What will you do in six months to lead through conflict and challenge?
For example: • Use figure 3.2 (page 62) to identify innovative practices you intend to model and implement in your building or district. Create expectations that these practices will be "the way we work here." Develop a progress-monitoring plan for six months to intentionally check in on the implementation of the practices.   • Use figure 3.3 (page 68) to consider your staff's believers, tweeners, survivors, and fundamentalists. Establish a plan to empower, motivate, educate, and clarify expectations as needed with each teacher. Use a six-month time frame to progress monitor your intentional focus on this work.
My ideas:

Chapter 4

Leading Change With Accountability

Effective leadership is not about making speeches or being liked; leadership is defined by results, not attributes.

—Peter Drucker

So far, we have taken you on a journey where the ultimate responsibility to lead is about making brave decisions, understanding your role as a coach, and ensuring that you seek every opportunity to build relationships, even when it means dealing with conflict. In this chapter, we explore the fine art of accepting the need to be accountable for your actions, and understanding how you lead based on results. Understanding how to lead change in your school or district is an essential step toward accountability; leaders accept that change is necessary and attention to what is changing (or not changing) creates accountability. In other words, you must know and understand your current reality and accept that if you seek improvements, it will require change. Being aware of what is and is not working (changing) leads to a greater understanding of your ability to be accountable and expect it from others.

In both our careers (and, honestly, some days in our personal lives), accountability has been a daunting task that we would rather avoid. Karen knows she avoided looking at her district provincial mathematics results for as long as she could because it was an area of definite need in her district. We both like the challenge of having an exercise accountability partner—someone who helps us get off the couch and out the door. We just don't always like the check-ins with this partner when we must be brutally honest about our progress!

Karen eventually had to look at the mathematics data, and Jeanne had to report her progress to her exercise accountability partner. We have both learned that accountability does not just mean a concern with numbers—*accountability* also means that you become self-disciplined enough to understand the current reality through evidence of your work. Leading from within requires the leader to know the score; in other words, there is no hiding from what story the data tell. It does take great self-discipline to focus on results, and as DuFour and colleagues state (2016), "Organizations do not focus on results: the people within them do—or they do not" (p. 89). The best-laid plans—school-improvement plans, district strategic plans, lesson plans, collaborative team unit plans, and so on—are only worth the paper written on when you model them through actions and expectations, and monitor these expectations for results. Let's look at how Mr. Hawkins, a brand-new high school principal, creates a sense of ownership and accountability by changing systems and practices, and is learning to monitor his tight expectations.

Principal Hawkins knew his daily decisions would drive the results of his school. How he acted, what he said, what evidence he used or did not use to inform practices, and what he followed up on as he monitored progress would impact his school's outcomes. He was excited to be named principal, but knew he had a daunting task as his school was in a state takeover position. Some needs had to be addressed, and changes were necessary. He also understood focusing on results is not just about accountability but also about knowing the proper steps to take at the right time.

During a coaching conversation with Principal Hawkins, Karen quickly surmised he was very intentional in his thinking and wanted to create a results-focused culture. It was important for him to notice what was happening around him and consider clarifying tight expectations. Principal Hawkins knew he had to build trust and understood this would involve a shared understanding of the work needed through clear expectations. Karen asked him to identify his priorities and establish his tight expectations, and then they worked together to create systematic ways to make change and, lastly, to progress monitor these expectations.

Reflection

As a leader, do you intentionally plan for change and focus on accountability around your expected changes? Is this a skill that needs more practice? How do you ask the right questions or notice what's happening around you? What are you looking for? How will you know when things are progressing or when you need to take corrective action? What next steps might you take to intentionally notice and account for successes and challenges?

Intentions Based on the Evidence of Results

As we write this chapter, many people are at home in self-isolation, as the COVID-19 pandemic marches through countries around the world. We do not know how long this will last or what the outcome will be, but we can see the need to be results focused in practices and how the misconceptions of what this means can frustrate people and cause confusion. There are opportunities, for example, to follow practices of countries or communities that stopped the spread of COVID-19 fairly quickly by looking at the actions they took and their results.

New Zealand is the best example of the alignment of intentional practice leading to positive results. For example, New Zealand began implementing its pandemic influenza plan in earnest in February 2020, which included preparing hospitals for an influx of patients and instituting border-control policies to delay the pandemic's arrival. As soon as the outbreak in China occurred, New Zealand closed its borders to China. The first New Zealand COVID-19 case was diagnosed on February 26, 2020, the same time that global agencies began reporting the SARS-CoV-2 infection was behaving more like a severe acute respiratory syndrome (SARS) than an influenza—giving investigators hope for containment. Because of a lack of testing and contact-tracing capability in mid-March, the country's leaders made a dramatic and critical switch in strategy: from mitigating the disease to eliminating it. A countrywide lockdown—Alert Level 4—was implemented on March 26, 2020. After five weeks, and with the number of new cases declining rapidly, New Zealand moved to Alert Level 3 for an additional two weeks, resulting in a total of seven weeks of what was essentially a national stay-at-home order. It was in early May 2020 when the last identified COVID-19 case was observed; with the patient placed in isolation, the country had ended its community spread. On June 8, New Zealand moved to Alert Level 1—in 103 days, they declared the pandemic over in the country. As of November 17, 2021, New Zealand has had 9,088 cases and only thirty-five deaths (New Zealand Ministry of Health, 2021). This demonstrates coronavirus-related mortality of seven per one million—one of the lowest reported rates among thirty-seven nations in the Organisation for Economic Co-operation and Development. New Zealand used scientific data and advice to plan for resurgences with various control measures, including early mass mask wearing. Additionally, the country's border-control strategies, as well as both community-based and individual case–based control measures, were overall effective in eliminating the virus's presence when mitigation was no longer feasible. Lastly, the country's people responded as a *community*, following their leader, Prime Minister Jacinda Ardern's, call for a unified "team of five million" as she provided empathic leadership and effectively communicated vital messages to the public (BBC News, 2020). She led from within and modeled a timely example of a results-focused culture. Throughout the pandemic, Prime Minister Ardern used (and continues to use) data to inform and account for her actions. She led the changes needed based on evidence, using a collaborative culture (and trusting that the evidence would compel others to follow). And, where there was misunderstanding or misinformation, she built common knowledge. She did not leave the will of her people or their ability to do what was needed to chance.

In early pandemic days, we observed less of a focus on the data and a slower response to evidence of community spread in other countries around the world. Some leaders were unable to explain the why of their decisions, which made it difficult for citizens to trust and follow their recommendations. As in all countries, New Zealand continues to experience surges in cases with COVID-19 variants. In January 2022, Prime Minister Ardern continued to lead by example, canceling her own wedding when the Omicron variant was found in New Zealand. With this announcement, she stated, "I am no different to, dare I say it, thousands of other New Zealanders who have had much more devastating impacts felt by the pandemic, the most gutting of which is the inability to be with a loved one sometimes when they are gravely ill. That will far, far outstrip any sadness I experience" (Needham, 2022).

Reflection

How can you apply Prime Minister Ardern's leadership style to your work as a leader in a school or district?

Knowledge: Skill and Will

As Principal Hawkins worked to build a culture focused on results for students, he considered the value of building his staff's knowledge, skills, and dispositions (or will) to effectively monitor and respond to student data. In his school, there was a long history of "this too shall pass." Historically, principals had come and gone, and the staff would avoid implementing expectations because they knew eventually, the principal would leave. Principal Hawkins, however, was determined to stay and improve the school, so he understood that *culture building* meant building capacity of the staff. He worked with positive intent, believing the teachers wanted the best results for students but just did not know how to get there.

The following scenario identifies a case where the disposition or *will* is evident, but there is a lack of knowledge and skills. Not attending to building knowledge and skills makes it difficult for those supporting or implementing the work to be effective. We believe as Principal Hawkins did—you cannot expect results if you have not provided the resources to build the skill set of your staff. We both have created anxiety when we didn't spend enough time on skills before expecting results.

Picture the following scenario: a superintendent hears about a promising response to intervention (RTI) conference coming to her town. She knows there is a need to implement a systemwide response to student needs through interventions. She looks at the program and decides she can pass on sending her staff and educate them herself. She skims through some readings and calls a principals' meeting. Her plan is titled "Implementing RTI as a District." She gives the principals an article to read by RTI expert Mike Mattos, and they watch a video together. She asks the principals how they feel about doing more work around RTI, and they all agree it is necessary. The superintendent shares a monitoring tool she wants the principals to use to account for the results they are getting with their new RTI plan. One principal raises his hand and says he heard a conference is coming to town and would like to go. He states that he doesn't understand enough about the three tiers of RTI and knows that, without this background knowledge, he isn't sure he can lead the work. The superintendent acknowledges his concerns but tells him the staff will figure it out as they go. The principals are a great group of willing leaders. They are ready to implement; however, they are unsure about what they are executing. More importantly, they lack the foundational understanding of implementing a successful response in a school. As a leader concerned about getting results, what might be more impactful steps to engage in with the goal of building skills and shared understanding?

For example, the superintendent in the previous scenario might have done the following.

1. Provide professional development to build a common understanding of RTI (conferences, book studies, videos, discussions, and action research). Principals, working in collaboration as a leadership team, read *Taking Action* over six months, building common understanding as they study together (Buffum, Mattos, & Malone, 2018).

2. Work with each school to build an inverted RTI pyramid (see figure 4.1, page 86), identifying what actions they feel are necessary for their school. Each principal shares the knowledge he or she gains from the book study and involves the school-based leadership team in building an RTI pyramid to support the implementation of the three tiers in their school.

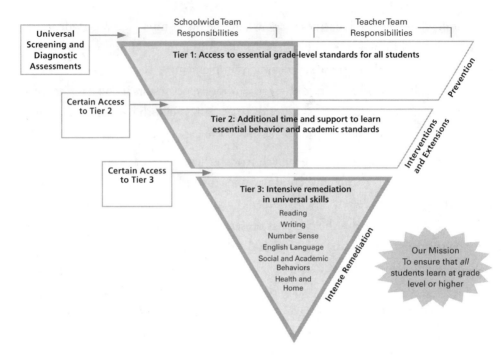

Source: Buffum et al., 2018, p. 18.

FIGURE 4.1: The RTI at Work™ pyramid.

3.   Develop a progress-monitoring tool or protocol with the principals to
     support the implementation of RTI—including progress monitoring
     the steps in the implementation before adding student data. Together,
     each school's leadership team (which includes the principal) agrees on
     how and when it will monitor the implementation of the three tiers of
     intervention in its school. The leadership team comes to a consensus on
     the document and their use of it as a team.

4.   Next steps are based on progress monitoring. The superintendent
     and the principals use the progress-monitoring tool as feedback to
     determine the next steps. This might include professional development
     for all schools or specific schools, supporting the implementation of
     a particular tier of intervention in the entire district, hiring more
     interventionists, providing more flexibility in master schedules for
     RTI, and so on.

In contrast with the superintendent, Principal Hawkins built an implementation
plan for his tight expectations, following the preceding four steps. He strategically
provided professional development on areas he identified as his priorities (high-yield
instructional expectations, collaborative team expectations, and evidence-based

interventions). He supported teachers both through classroom observations and feedback and in collaborative teams. He was able to provide resources and support as teachers built timely, effective interventions. Principal Hawkins understood the value of progress monitoring and created easy-to-use tools for the progress monitoring of his expectations. His school's guiding coalition (or leadership team) spent time each month celebrating successes (even if minimal) and planning next steps based on data. Principal Hawkins knows that school improvement is a journey and requires diligent, consistent work. He has the systems in place to build a shared understanding of expectations, and he is willing to face the current reality through progress monitoring.

Figure 4.2 provides an example and offers an opportunity for you to reflect on more intentional actions to create a results-driven and focused culture through skill development. See the example in the first row and use the blank spaces in the reproducible version at **go.SolutionTree.com/PLCbooks** to create your scenarios, indicating the problem, results you desire, and your actions to support the results.

The Problem	Results Desired	Actions That Support the Results Through Skill Building
My principals are willing to implement RTI to support student learning, but they do not have the knowledge and skills yet to accomplish this work.	Increased student achievement as we focus student by student and skill by skill in our response through interventions as a district	Provide professional development to build a common understanding of RTI (conferences, book studies, videos, discussions, action research). Work with each school to build an RTI pyramid, identifying what actions staff feel are necessary for their school. Develop a progress-monitoring tool or protocol with the principals to support the implementation of RTI—progress monitor steps in implementation before adding student data. The next steps are based on progress monitoring.

FIGURE 4.2: Identifying skill-building actions to support a results-focused culture.

*Visit **go.SolutionTree.com/PLCbooks** for a free reproducible version of this figure.*

We Don't Know What We Don't Know

The previous superintendent's RTI scenario focuses on failed implementation due to a lack of staff knowledge and skills regarding the *why* and *how* (not because the principals were unwilling). Karen's example of trying to implement the PLC process in her district was very similar. Her principals and teachers were primarily willing; however, deep implementation requires attention to capacity building (skill) to get the results she envisioned. Without building the capacity, there will be a trickle-down effect on the entire system, causing more roadblocks along the way. For example, an entire school staff may think they are doing the very best they can with their instructional practices to meet the needs of their students. They do not have the knowledge and skills to help them consider different ways to approach teaching and learning. In addition, they are not collaborating to share ideas and practices, and their leaders do not expect them to read or study examples of other successful schools or districts. Essentially, there is no PLC process in their school. They go about their business, doing the very best they can with what they know to do. They do not have exposure to experts or principals who have had the opportunity to build their knowledge about best practices. Their district continuously reminds them of their poor results with students, but they genuinely do not know what to do to change this trajectory. *They don't know what they don't know.*

In his book, *The Advantage*, author Patrick Lencioni (2012) explains the many benefits for leaders to pay attention to the health of their organization. Lencioni (2012) shares a way to look at organizational health:

> See it as the multiplier of intelligence. The healthier an organization is, the more of its intelligence it can tap into and use. Most organizations exploit only a fraction of the knowledge, experience, and intellectual capital that is available to them. But the healthier ones tap into almost all of it. (p. 11)

As we think about leading schools and districts from within, we recognize the health of an organization is dependent on the leader's willingness and ability to recognize what is known or unknown. Understanding your staff's current level of knowledge, skill, and will provides opportunities to develop, share, and empower expertise within your system. As trust was building during Principal Hawkins's first months as the school's leader, he noticed teachers who wanted to lead. He formed a guiding coalition (leadership team) and was pleasantly surprised at the expertise around the table. The teachers were excited for Principal Hawkins to ask their opinions on the next steps when looking at data, and he soon learned who truly understood quality instruction and intervention planning. Once the teachers on his collaborative teams understood the process, they were willing to share their expertise as they developed assessments and next steps for students. Principal Hawkins understood that to create the changes needed to improve his school, he would need to continue building his staff's capacity. He could not do this work alone. He also recognized he had resisters who were unwilling or unable to do the work. As he was building the capacity of those who could lead, he addressed the skills (and will) others needed. This intentional focus created a healthy organization.

Worldwide authority on educational reform Michael Fullan (2006) reminds us:

> Capacity building is defined as any strategy that increases the collective effectiveness of a group to raise the bar and close the gap of student learning. . . . Most theories of change are weak on capacity building and that is one of the key reasons why they fall short. (p. 9)

Fullan (2006) continues:

> An emphasis on accountability by itself produces negative pressure: pressure that doesn't motivate and that doesn't get to capacity building. Positive pressure is pressure that does motivate, that is palpably fair and reasonable and does come accompanied by resources for capacity building. The more one invests in capacity building, the more one has the right to expect greater performance. The more one focuses on results fairly—comparing like schools, using data over multiple years, providing targeted support for improvement—the more that motivational leverage can be used. (p. 9)

Considering Fullan's (2006) wise statements, it makes sense that Principal Hawkins focused much of his first year on understanding and building the skills of his teachers. In fact, as a first-year principal, he had good instincts about how he would only focus on accountability once people understood expectations and were capable of doing the work needed to improve the school. In Lencioni's (2012) view, Principal Hawkins was taking care of the health of his organization.

As you focus on accountability and results, leading from within requires attention to this human capital. As we coach in districts and schools, we too often observe expectations for changes to happen with little attention to staff needs. We also know it takes many messages, modeling, coaching, observations, and support to build staff capacity. Starting with those who understand and building their ability to shine and share are excellent first steps. Small wins and celebrations of what is working are extremely helpful for others to see what your expectations look like when they implement them effectively. Pause here and reflect on what you notice in your district and school. How is this impacting your ability to lead with a focus on results?

> ### Reflection
>
> Who are your rock stars? Are you empowering them by sharing their skills and expertise? What are your small wins and celebrations? How can you build more capacity through *noticing and acknowledging*?

Change for Results

As educators lean toward accountability and focus on school improvement, they become *change agents*. Everything we have addressed so far in this chapter (and, in fact, in most of this book) is about the changing practices of yourself and others. We know this requires time and attention to detail. We also know it takes planning and acknowledging what has to change to get your desired results.

Reeves (2009) writes, "Failure in change strategies need not be inevitable. In fact, it is avoidable if change leaders will balance their sense of urgency with a more thoughtful approach to implementing change" (p. 7). Wanting to see results is a great start, but the rubber hits the road when leaders, as Reeves (2009) describes, take a *thoughtful approach to implement change*.

As previously discussed, implementing a cultural shift toward results requires an understanding of what unknowns to address. Intentionally noticing the difference between *will* and *skill* as obstacles and being well aware of the expertise and leadership within your staff will take you far as a leader of change. Do you have an understanding of what teachers do not know about instruction, assessment, and intervention practices? Have you examined what is working, so you know what to continue to do? How do you model and support what you expect? In other words, leading change requires a relentless effort. Use the following guiding questions to inform that effort.

- **Understand:** What do you want to accomplish for results, and what do your staff and students need to get there?

- **Educate:** What do you need to learn, teach, and understand to change your practices?

- **Support:** What coaching, ongoing professional development, mentoring, observations, and feedback will you need to support the changes?

- **Monitor:** How will you progress monitor your desired changes?

- **Adjust:** How will you know what you are doing is working or not working? Are you closer to results? What do you need to do differently?

Figure 4.3 provides a visual of this cycle.

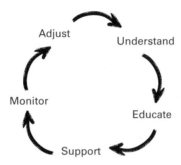

FIGURE 4.3: Illustration of the continuous change cycle for a results-focused culture.

The next step is to *repeat*; start over again (and again) until you achieve your results. Take a few minutes for reflection and use figure 4.4 to practice thoughtful planning for how you might respond to the guiding questions for each of the steps in this cycle for a results-focused culture.

Step in the Cycle for Continuous Change for a Results-Focused Culture	Guiding Questions	Your Notes (What you know, don't know, or wonder about)	Your Intended Next Steps
Understand	What do you want to accomplish for results, and what do your staff and students need to get there?		

FIGURE 4.4: Practicing the continuous change cycle for a results-focused culture.

continued →

Step in the Cycle for Continuous Change for a Results-Focused Culture	Guiding Questions	Your Notes (What you know, don't know, or wonder about)	Your Intended Next Steps
Educate	What do you need to learn, teach, and understand to change your practices?		
Support	What coaching, ongoing professional development, mentoring, observations, and feedback will you need to support the changes?		
Monitor	How will you progress monitor your desired changes?		
Adjust	How will you know what you are doing is working or not working? Are you closer to results? What do you need to do differently?		

Visit **go.SolutionTree.com/PLCbooks** *for a free reproducible version of this figure.*

In chapter 3 (page 55), we shared that Kotter's (2008, 2012) eight steps of change begin with a sense of urgency and end with changes embedded deeply in the organization's culture. In our coaching, we often use figure 4.5 to help leaders understand the requirements in the change process (Ambrose, 1987). We know this research is dated; however, during coaching, we find it impactful for leaders to understand the requirements and the impact of their absence. When you remove any one of these requirements, it results in an obstacle to change. As a new principal with many changes to implement, Principal Hawkins had to be careful not to go too fast and miss any opportunities to build these requirements. He would be the first to admit he missed a few steps and had to take a step back when he saw anxiety, frustration, and slow implementation. Figure 4.6 (page 94) helped Principal Hawkins revisit his implementation plans and reboot his efforts. After you review figure 4.5, use figure 4.6 to reflect on a change you are trying to make toward better results. Are any of the requirements missing? What can you do to thoughtfully tighten your practices?

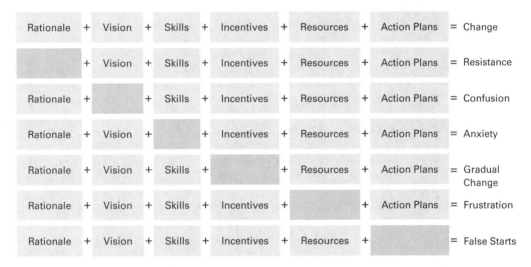

Source: Adapted from Ambrose, 1987.

FIGURE 4.5: Ambrose's requirements for managing complex change.

As you reflect on a change you are working to implement, consider the requirements for change (Ambrose, 1987). How are you addressing each during implementation? What action plans do you need to ensure change?

What change are you working to create?	How have you explained and built understanding of the rationale?	How have you explained and built an understanding of the vision?	What skills are necessary, and how are you addressing them?	How are the benefits of the change understood? What incentives support this?	What resources do you need or use?	How intentional is your action plan, and what are the necessary next steps based on this reflection?

FIGURE 4.6: Reflection—requirements for change.

Visit go.SolutionTree.com/PLCbooks for a free reproducible version of this figure.

Data *Rich* or Information *Poor*

Educational leaders are no strangers to data. However, it can feel like information overload as data sets from many data points appear in your inbox or on your desk. On any given day, a superintendent might be required to know the arrival times of their buses, student and staff attendance, expenditures for electricity, maintenance, and of course, the student achievement results for the district. At the school level, some of the same data points are available, and during our coaching visits, principals often tell us they are too overwhelmed to know where to start. As presented previously in this chapter, accountability requires an intentional focus on the change process, and change begins with an understanding of the story your data unveil. During coaching sessions, the amount of data school and district leaders are expected to understand is often overwhelming.

An excellent first step is to consider the data you need to understand your current reality in the most critical areas to impact student learning. What data points will help you understand successes and challenges within your system that need attention? What data points do you have (or perhaps need to have) that will paint an accurate picture of your situation? With an intentional focus on these data points first, leaders understand changes that must take place. With this baseline and action plans for change, how and when you will need to progress monitor are subsequent step decisions. Having guidelines or rules to use is a great way to simplify the use of data. One set of guidelines we introduce our leaders to is from former Superintendent Thomas Many (2009), who offers the following steps to begin using data to inform next steps. Leaders can create tools to support the management, process, and discussion of data. Many (2009) recommends ensuring data use meets the following criteria.

1. **Easily managed and accessible:** Leaders ensure data are *easily managed and accessible* for district and school leaders, guiding coalitions, and collaborative teams to use. This is done by creating a data-collection tool for sharing and displaying data results.

2. **Purposefully arranged:** When creating a data-collection tool, keep in mind data need to be *purposefully arranged* in a format that is complete, accurate, and straightforward. Displaying data in user-friendly tables, charts, or graphs helps leaders and teachers maintain focus on results and limit potential distractions, and allows them to see the information from the data in a timely and effective manner.

3. **Publicly discussed:** Leaders should embark on creating a safe space and a process of *publicly discussing* results after collecting all relative data. To create an environment conducive for sharing data, advisor and author Joellen Killion (2008) suggests using a data-analysis protocol that "keeps the focus on issues rather than people, engages people in an appreciative inquiry approach rather than a deficit approach to a situation, and results in a plan of action that energizes and motivates people" (p. 7).

After Many's (2009) district began using these guidelines, his successors added the following step.

4. **Action oriented:** When data protocols are *action oriented*, leaders can quickly establish results-focused goals and action plans. Actions include establishing next steps and a progress-monitoring plan for implementation so adjustments made along the way are timely and responsive. Those steps build processes toward the results you desire.

Leading from within requires a continuous focus on knowing your current reality and wisely changing as needed to accomplish your goals. Use the data protocol in figure 4.7 to consider how to implement or adjust.

Protocol steps	What this looks like in practice	Your next steps to implement or adjust practice
1. Easily managed and accessible	Leaders ensure data are *easily managed and accessible* for district and school leaders, guiding coalitions, and collaborative teams to use. This is done by creating a data-collection tool for sharing and displaying data results.	
2. Purposefully arranged	When creating a data-collection tool, keep in mind data need to be *purposefully arranged* in a format that is complete, accurate, and straightforward. Displaying data in user-friendly tables, charts, or graphs helps leaders and teachers maintain focus on results, limit potential distractions, and allows them to see the information from the data in a timely and effective manner.	

| 3. Publicly discussed | Leaders should embark on creating a safe space and a process of *publicly discussing* results after collecting all relative data. To create an environment conducive for sharing data, Killion (2008) suggests using a data-analysis protocol that "keeps the focus on issues rather than people, engages people in an appreciative inquiry approach rather than a deficit approach to a situation, and results in a plan of action that energizes and motivates people" (p. 7). | |
| 4. Action oriented | When data protocols are *action oriented*, leaders can quickly establish results-focused goals and action plans. Actions include establishing next steps and a progress-monitoring plan for implementation so adjustments made along the way are timely and responsive. Those steps build processes toward the results you desire. | |

Source: Adapted from Kildeer Countryside Community Consolidated School District 96; Many, 2009.

FIGURE 4.7: Four-step data protocol.

*Visit **go.SolutionTree.com/PLCbooks** for a free reproducible version of this figure.*

As discussed earlier in this chapter, it is essential to identify what you want to accomplish and align your change actions to get you there. Using data protocols, such as the example in figure 4.7 or other progress-monitoring tools, will help you understand the implementation level of your expected changes. Without progress monitoring, it is challenging to understand what is happening or why something fails to impact. Leading from within requires a relentless focus on knowing the current reality and accepting that you might need to adjust actions and plans. One great way to progress monitor is through the use of SMART goals (Conzemius & O'Neill, 2014; O'Neill & Conzemius, 2006). Let's look at how these goals help you lead and account for changes.

SMART Goals

As we coach in schools and districts, educators ask us, "Is it essential for collaborative teams or school administrators to set SMART goals and monitor progress toward them?" Unfortunately, it is a step in the PLC process that is too often left out or, more commonly, we find educators write but then forget the goals until the time comes to update a school-improvement plan. Being goal focused *and* bringing these goals to life mean constantly revisiting and progress monitoring. It also means educators take every opportunity to revisit instruction, intervention, and assessment plans when SMART goals are unmet. When you consider a results-focused culture, it must include goal setting and progress monitoring toward these goals.

Let's review what goal setting looks like in districts and schools. Consultants and educators Jan O'Neill and Anne E. Conzemius (2006, 2014) define *SMART goals* as strategic and specific, measurable, attainable, results oriented, and time bound. These goals help focus your work on the same outcome. You can set SMART goals for both process and results at all levels. For example, a school district leadership team might establish a process goal to change the equity practices of the district: *By the end of the 2020–2021 school year, all school board policies will be reviewed and revised to support equitable practices in all schools.* This process goal will help the district work toward more equitable services for all students, which is the overall result it wants. Write student-achievement SMART goals at all levels as well. A school guiding coalition needs to consider the data it is using to measure student achievement and write its SMART goal with that achievement measurement in mind. For example, Jeanne's school district writes SMART goals based on student-growth data. Staff derive student-growth and achievement projections from each student's previous year's scores on assessments educators administer to all students every year, including the Northwest Evaluation Association's (NWEA) Measures of Academic Progress (MAP) assessment, the end-of-year state assessment, and other universal screeners. Based on the projections, some students will not meet grade-level proficiency on MAP and the state assessment. A SMART goal based on these data might look like this: *Students projected not to meet grade-level proficiency in mathematics will exceed projections as measured by the end-of-year state mathematics assessment.* The SMART goal for students projected to meet proficiency would read this way: *Students projected to meet grade-level proficiency in mathematics will meet or exceed projections as measured by the end-of-year state assessment.* In both cases, the winter and spring MAP assessments and team common formative and summative assessments monitor progress. An overall school or district goal might look like this: *For each school's most significant area of need by subject (mathematics or English language arts) and grade, overall growth will* exceed *projections for that subject in that grade. For the other subject in each grade, the grade level will* meet *or* exceed *the projections.*

Teams write goals this way after recognizing that the process of setting goals with increments of growth or achievement they identified was based on random, not statistically based percentages of growth or proficiency. To illustrate, previously, teams wrote goals like: *Students who are projected* not *to meet grade-level proficiency in mathematics will increase proficiency by 10 percent or increase from 52 percent to 65 percent.* Why 10 percent? Why a 13-percentage point increase? What is the statistical significance of these increases? As Jeanne's team considered this process, measuring progress student by student with growth targets as the focus made more sense. Consider how you will measure progress and what systems you have in place to help you measure progress effectively. The key is to ensure your goals have the attributes of SMART goals—strategic and specific, measurable, attainable, results oriented, and time bound.

> ### Reflection
>
> What is the power in setting SMART goals to establish the results you expect?

Leaders use SMART goals at the state or provincial, district, and school levels as a tool to understand intended outcomes, progress monitor the journey, and celebrate small and big wins. Goals should be aligned throughout the system; in other words, they should set student individual learning goals that directly correlate all the way up to school, district, and state expectations. Ownership of learning is reflected in ownership of SMART goals. Each step along the way provides an accumulated focus on results and accountability. Consider the analogy of flying a plane in the next section to deepen your understanding of the need for consistent alignment of goals within your system.

Flying the Plane

When consultant and coach Dennis King begins his work with schools, he carefully examines their work, intentionally noticing if these efforts bring them the results they want. The guiding question is always, Is the school improving? King explains:

> To understand a results-focused culture, SMART goals must be seen as the process to get the results, not the product of the work. Evidence (several data points) informs us of what the current reality is. Then goals are set to help us understand the results that we want. (personal communication, March 28, 2020)

King adds, "If teachers are going to own the process and have felt a need for a results-focused culture, SMART goals must be established with them that are closely going to impact their classroom practices" (personal communication, March 28, 2020). King uses the analogy of a plane to understand goal setting:

> Think about a plane flying at 30,000 feet; those are the data that describe and compare students to other students nationally or internationally like PISA, SAT, or other national and international tests. As the plane begins its descent, the 10,000-ft. data represent what states and provinces want to know about their students. As the plane gets closer to landing, we can see the data that districts use—benchmark, screeners, etc., and lastly, when the plane is on the ground, we have the data that collaborative teams and individual teachers have in classrooms—formative assessments and summative assessments for units. (personal communication, March 28, 2020)

Ensuring a Successful Landing

As a passenger on this plane, you want processes in place at all levels of elevation to ensure a successful outcome; however, you cannot deny that once the plane lands, passengers often let out a sigh of relief, a smile appears on many faces, and sometimes passengers even clap their hands. The pilot is often at the door as they exit, acknowledging them and saying "goodbye." The result of a safe landing is all they want. Before the flight, the crew performs safety checks, and throughout the flight, the pilot and crew progress monitor and take action toward a safe landing. People trust the pilot has the knowledge and competence to do the work necessary to meet the goal of landing the plane. Training, observations, and practice have been part of the preparation. Applying this learning during the journey gets the pilot, crew, and passengers to a successful and safe landing.

As we learned more and more about school improvement, we often heard our mentor Rick DuFour state that "leaders are often flying the plane as it's being built." They make changes and adjustments as the journey continues. As you build your plane, intentionally notice what you must do to align SMART goals throughout your system and how you will check for progress along the way. How are you going to account for actions? What data will assist you in changing directions or tightening expectations? What requirements of change have you missed in your planning? And how can you set SMART goals to help you have a laser-like focus on the changes you want? Every crew member knows his or her role on the plane, and you see the same practices in place time and time again on flights, no matter what airline you fly. These practices get the desired results—that final goal of a safe landing. When you think of school improvement, see a parallel to flying the plane. Leaders need to plan well, understand their roles, and have aligned systems and practices in place to ensure the school or district successfully achieves the end goals.

Celebrating, Celebrating, Celebrating

Leaders with a positive mindset and an understanding of the use of SMART goals foundationally build a culture of success and recognize that small wins are just as important as *award-winning* days. As stated earlier, progress monitoring SMART goals as part of consistent practices at every level of the system (including student-owned learning goals) provides wonderful opportunities to celebrate growth. This also requires leaders to have an intentional awareness of cultural shifts as they happen and then bring attention to the efforts that guide the changes. As districts and schools develop a PLC process as the "way we work here," a culture of shared leadership and ownership creates many opportunities to notice and celebrate together. As you lead from within, you bring more specific and intentional celebrations to life. You understand it is not enough to say, "We are doing a great job." A results-focused culture deserves the recognition of what is causing the great work and how staff are getting there. For example, when collaborative teams meet their SMART goal, celebrate this publicly with staff. This sends the message that data and a results-driven culture are valued. It also helps potential resisters see evidence of effectiveness. Err on the side of too much intentional and specific information about successful implementation and results rather than general statements that paint a rosy picture but do not focus on how your culture has changed. Principal Sarah Stobaugh of Morrilton Intermediate School in Arkansas celebrates the collaborative culture of her school with her entire staff through email and social media in the following example. She knows this culture took time to build, and she also knows the staff are now seeing the benefits of true collaboration:

> I hope all of you are well and not going too stir crazy just yet. I want
> to tell you what I have seen this week and share another testament
> of why the PLC process is the ONLY way to work. As we got the very

short notice that our schools were closing down, we watched educators and parents across our state (and country) panic. While other
teachers may have been scrambling to figure out what to do and
feeling completely overwhelmed and somewhat alone, our teachers
remained calm. They had worked together all year long and continued
to function as a team when they got the news their instruction was
about to look different. We had planned all year, we had tracked our
data, and we had a very clear idea of what each student needed as
we sent them home to continue to learn in a completely different setting. Because our teachers truly believe ALL means ALL, they set up
a clear way to communicate and began to record videos for students
to watch to feel connected, not just their own. While some teachers
came to the schools during the day to deliver lunches for those in
need, they knew their team was home answering questions for all
students. They continue to work together from home in this uncertain
time. Our students will still have access to all teachers, not just their
own, because that is what is best for students. They are adjusting
their "work hours" to be available to those students whose parents
are not home during the day and may have questions after 3:30 p.m.
because that is what is best for kids. This is why the PLC must become
a culture and not simply a protocol. . . . because in these very uncertain times, we are still functioning under the values that represent the
PLC process. If we had not been through this work and learned under
the guidance of the very best "in the business," I feel certain that
we would be falling apart right about now, but we're not; we are still
working as a team to serve ALL students no matter the circumstance.
(personal communication, S. Stobaugh, May 17, 2020)

Wrap-Up

When times are challenging, if you have created a results-driven collaborative culture, it will show up, survive, and be strong. However, if you have done *PLC lite*—in
other words, you have teams and data, but you do not have authentically shared ownership of student learning—the culture may fall apart during challenges. Leading
from within to build strong accountability practices deepens the PLC process as you
take the time to build a shared understanding of the purpose of the work and intentionally create opportunities for both skill and will to develop. As a leader, you continuously monitor progress, adjusting as required. As you end this chapter, use the

reflective tool (page 104) to review your practices and create plans to increase your impact. Chapter 5 (page 107) explores the world beyond the walls of the school or district offices. What leadership lessons can you learn from others? How are corporation leaders leading from within? Consider your practices and your current reality as you use the reflection tool to identify your next steps.

Six-Sentence Summary

Leading from within requires the leader to know the score—there is no hiding from the story the data tell. The best-laid plans (school-improvement plans, district strategic plans, lesson plans, collaborative team unit plans, and so on) are only worth the paper they are written on when you model them through actions and expectations, and monitor these expectations for results. Leading change within your system requires intentional, accountable actions. As you build a culture focused on results for students, consider the value of building your staff's knowledge, skills, and dispositions (or will) to monitor and respond to student data effectively. Implementing a cultural shift through change includes goal setting and progress monitoring to determine what is working and what is not. Every journey has a beginning, stops along the way, and an end or goal, and leading from within requires a personal commitment to knowing the beginning, monitoring the signs along the way, and understanding the desired outcomes.

Making an Impact in Six: Leading Change With Accountability

The following six ideas provide opportunities for further reflection and action. We provide three reflections on what great leaders do and avoid doing to gain focus, as well as three considerations for how to make an impact in six minutes, six weeks, and six months to guide your leadership planning and practice.

Thoughtful Leaders Do . . .	Thoughtful Leaders Avoid . . .
1. Take time to thoughtfully understand and plan professional development and support based on what staff know and do not know to get the results they expect.	Assuming staff members understand how to get the results they expect without providing professional development opportunities and checking in to coach, support, and provide feedback
Current reality and next steps:	
2. Create opportunities to celebrate and recognize both the skill and will of staff by sharing artifacts and specific details that create awareness, shared pride, and ownership.	Not finding the time and effort to notice the details and acknowledge how the culture is changing
Current reality and next steps:	
3. Empower staff to lead by modeling, coaching, and sharing expectations for a results-driven focus. This includes hosting data talks with individual teachers, collaborative teams, and students.	Spending too much time with top-down leadership; not taking the time to explain and show *why* and *how* their expectations will build a results-driven culture
Current reality and next steps:	

4. What will you do in six minutes to lead change with accountability?

For example:

- Ask yourself, "Am I clear about what results I expect and what is important to me as a leader? How do I communicate these goals to staff? What would staff say if someone asked them what the expected results are for our organization?" Talk with some of your staff and students to determine the answers if you are unsure.

- Intentionally participate in one collaborative team meeting to observe the use of data in determining the next steps for students. Provide support and coaching to deepen conversations as needed.

My ideas:

5. What will you do in six weeks to lead change with accountability?

For example:

- Create a professional development plan based on staff needs so they learn and understand how to work toward the expected results. Ensure this plan includes follow-up observations, coaching, support, and feedback, and intentionally builds in time for you to connect with staff members. Create time for follow-up professional learning as needed for collaborative teams and individual teachers. Develop a progress-monitoring tool that will allow you to measure changes being made toward your results. Report out on this progress to staff and adjust your plans as needed.

- Develop a progress-monitoring plan that includes ongoing data meetings with teachers and leaders. Intentionally seek to understand the information in the data to inform next steps. Ask clarifying questions and build a shared understanding of the use of data, and celebrate small and big wins.

My ideas:

6. What will you do in six months to lead change with accountability?

For example:

- Create data walls (virtual or physical) that provide a visual of progress. Include staff as you progress monitor and update data walls. Find every opportunity to celebrate growth and achievement, and use the data walls to inform next steps.

- Implement student–data tracking expectations for all students. As you visit classrooms, engage students in results-driven conversations using their own goals and data. Host a family night for students to explain their progress through their data-tracking products.

My ideas:

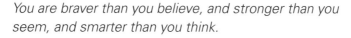

Chapter 5

Going the Extra Mile (and Looking After Yourself)

You are braver than you believe, and stronger than you seem, and smarter than you think.

—A. A. Milne, Christopher Robin to Winnie-the-Pooh

Leadership is exhausting. It brings out the best and worst in you. It demands a great deal of your time and attention. It gets in the way of having fun. It seems like too much work. We understand that bringing your *A game* to the table every day requires courageous determination, focused intentions, and lots of energy. However, for whom you serve, your "good enough" is not enough. Leadership requires a more profound commitment to strive to be better, and this indeed draws on your ability to lead from within.

If you are a leader reading this, we know there have been days you just wanted to stay in bed. There have been times when it seemed like a better idea is to just keep driving rather than go into the building, and when hours and minutes stretched on forever. What is it that gets you out of bed? How do you get out of the car and ready yourself for the day? What are your strategies to stop looking at your watch and be present, no matter the situation? Leading from within stretches leaders to give their all—and even more at times. Finding the inner strength to continuously seek improvement for yourself, your school, and your district requires the grit and focus that come from your heart and soul. If someone isn't going to light your fire, how do you draw on your intrinsic motivation? What motivates you and inspires you to dig deep and find the energy, enthusiasm, and commitment to lead? This chapter shares our ideas and experiences for ways to dig deep, create the positive mindset, and mostly, find the *grit* you need to lead. We invite you to consider developing personal and leadership abilities to go the extra mile.

What foundationally got you into leadership? Do you remember a moment or event that influenced you to lead? Was it an inspiring person who modeled how impactful outstanding leadership can be? Perhaps it was the opposite experience— working with someone who didn't lead, and a lack of direction and support negatively affected you. Were you born into a family of leaders? Did others expect you to lead? Or did someone who believes in you mentor and coach you to take on a leadership role? Whatever your journey, and despite how much experience you now have (or do not have), leadership constantly requires an ability to find the strength and courage to lead from within. Let's look at some ways to build this ability.

Making a Personal Commitment

In our quest to help you understand the truth about leadership being hard work, first think about the personal commitment to lead an organization or even a team of two. Intentionally or unintentionally, you commit to lead systems, effective practices, and, most importantly, people. We daresay it is always better when you intentionally recognize the commitment leadership requires; however, leaders often find themselves in situations where stepping up to lead is the right thing to do, and it naturally happens. Can you think of a sports team you watched and noticed what happens when the bench players step up? A star falls ill or is injured and, without any warning, a young player comes in off the bench, intentionally or unintentionally personally commits to doing his or her best, and leads the team to victory. For example, at the 2020 Summer Olympic Games, American gymnast Jade Carey took the floor for her incredible performance in the women's gymnastics all-around final, replacing Olympic champion Simone Biles. One day before, Carey was not competing in this Olympic event. She finished in eighth place, a result she and all the United States are proud of. Biles and her teammates cheered Carey on from the stands. Following the event, Carey stated, "I feel really proud of myself for how I was able to step in at the last minute and compete" (as cited in Galofaro, 2021).

Opportunities to lead are all around you; it can naturally happen when needed or sadly, avoided at all costs. It is most frustrating and challenging to observe when a person has positional leadership (that is, the title and power) but does not personally commit. Leadership is absent despite the authority that comes with the position. The corner office and parking space are full, but the person tasked with leading is not accomplishing the real work. Despite accepting the position, the genuine commitment and responsibility to the position are not there.

As leadership coaches and lifelong educators, we understand leading from within requires intentionally acknowledging a personal commitment to accept the role and responsibility of leadership. In other words, we have enough self-discipline to understand the importance and value we bring to the positions we hold. As a leader, you must accept this responsibility. Ideally, this commitment begins before you apply for a position. A great preinterview or interview question candidates are often asked is to reflect on their *why*. If you are conducting the interview, give serious consideration to how a candidate answers this question. And, if you are the interviewee, provide excellent care in articulating your *why*. The reason for seeking a new position should demonstrate a personal commitment to values, people, and responsibility. In your daily life, it is great practice to find the time to reflect and consider *why* you are leading and *how* you accepted the responsibility to commit your time, energy, and resources to the role of leader. It is OK to feel this commitment waver from time to time; finding a strategy that brings it back to life is an essential daily practice.

The last thing we want to do in this chapter is scare you away from leadership. However, we want you to face the brutal fact: leadership is a personal commitment and does require continuous renewal. In fact, as the newness of a position wears off, that is when to take the deep dive to lead from within; the renewal of a personal commitment is critically important. Use figure 5.1 to reflect on your promise. Write a personal commitment statement for yourself. What intentional steps can you take to commit or reconfirm?

Personal Commitment Statement to Lead From Within	Next Steps to Commit or Reconfirm
Example: I will not stop leading when the work is tiring, boring, or frustrating, and I don't know what to do next.	I will begin each morning with reflection and establish a positive mindset intentionally focused on my priorities for the day.

FIGURE 5.1: Reflection—personal commitment.

*Visit **go.SolutionTree.com/PLCbooks** for a free reproducible version of this figure.*

Finding Grit

In her best-selling book, *Grit*, author Angela Duckworth (2016) describes *grit* as the combination of passion and perseverance for long-term goals. She explains *passion* is not intensity or enthusiasm held briefly; it is about endurance. *Perseverance* is the ability to overcome setbacks, put in the challenging work, and complete tasks and projects you start. Chapter 1 of our first book, *Leading With Intention*, details the need to prioritize and focus despite distractors (Spiller & Power, 2019). As we coach leaders, we witness their authentic desire to remain focused; however, we also experience the struggle that transpires without the grit to endure. In our opinion, what separates successful and unsuccessful attempts at staying true to priorities comes from within, as passion and perseverance become interdependent. Leading from within and going the extra mile (or miles) happen when passion exists and you persevere despite the obstacles. In other words, you feel passionate about the task, project, and next steps, and you persist in taking action, follow-through, implementation, and so on, to reach the goals and outcomes. We like to compare this to going on a long road trip. You are passionate about the journey and getting to the destination. Still, it will require continuous attention to detail to ensure you reach your destination—being well planned and prepared, driving safely, knowing where you are going, and putting in the long hours of driving that will get you to your destination—one mile at a time.

Have you ever had someone say to you, "I couldn't do that" or "I don't know how you do it"? If you are leading, you are doing magical things every day that others marvel at. We know it may feel like you have superhuman powers some days, and even when you have a challenging day, others around you see the job gets done. Grit takes over. Your inner strength pushes you through the distractors and roadblocks, and you are one step closer to your desired goals. School and district improvement are not linear; some days will feel messy (well, honestly, most will), and you will not always see the benefits of your hard work. It takes patience and time to create change.

As with other leadership skills, we believe developing grit is intentional. You don't have to be born with natural tendencies to persevere and lead passionately from within. You can purposefully go about the business of increasing your ability to do this. In our leadership journeys, we have both developed strategies to lean on. Karen used the acronym TOTAL to provide a step-by-step consistent process of reflection, ownership, and action. Use figure 5.2 to review Karen's TOTAL process and our suggested strategies to help when you need the interrelatedness of passion and perseverance.

The *TOTAL* Picture	Strategies	Notes and Next Steps
T*hink*	Reflect, review, revise, and *think*. Great leaders understand the need to continuously think about what they are doing to get where they want to go. Consider your options, know the path to success, and figure out how to get there. Do not chance this. Continuously reflecting, reviewing, revising, and thinking will help you feel more successful as you move toward your goals.	
O*wn*	Accept responsibility for the leadership work you need to achieve goals. *Own* the work and build your plan around personal ownership. This does not mean you do not share leadership, but it does mean you take on the responsibility to lead.	
T*ime*	Commit *time* to what has to be done. Consider how much time you will need—and plan for this. Carve out time in the day for intentional work that will lead to desired outcomes. This moves you from *saying* to *doing*.	
A*ccount*	Honestly *account* for your actions. Establish personal accountability check-ins; monitor how you spent your time, what you focus on with your time, and if you know if you are making change. Hope is not a strategy, and great leaders understand leading with results in mind.	
L*earn*	Be a continuous learner. *Learn* from your mistakes. Learn by doing. Lead through a learning lens. Be a student of what you want to accomplish. This helps you feel confident as you push forward.	

FIGURE 5.2: The *TOTAL* picture.

*Visit **go.SolutionTree.com/PLCbooks** for a free reproducible version of this figure.*

Modeling What You Expect

As we continue to provide leadership coaching, we often ask leaders to reflect with two fundamental questions: (1) "What are you doing during the day?" and (2) "Where do you spend your time?" If you are reading this book and one of us has coached you, you know the drill. We want you to face the brutal facts. We need to know and help you see that genuinely leading from within means modeling your expectations. It is never enough to plan, talk, and think. The old phrase, "Actions speak louder than words," comes to mind.

Briefly, what separates leaders who can go the extra mile versus those who do *leadership lite* is what you model and take action on. Earning the respect and trust of others creates opportunities to have an impact. This comes from when you do the work. You take the necessary steps, show up at critical times, and use your grit to stay true to your expectations. Being true to your priorities requires careful attention to your non-negotiable expectations or having tight expectations that guide your work and the work of those you lead. For example, in Lee County, Arkansas, Superintendent Willie Murdock led a shared leadership conversation with her district's guiding coalition to create tight expectations for the 2021–2022 school year. If she wanted to make a change, Superintendent Murdock understood she would need to have a consensus on the most critical work and districtwide expectations. The guiding coalition agreed on three priorities for the school year and then created ten tight expectations for the district. As Karen worked with the team, she observed members' passion for the improvement they wanted to make and the personal commitment that each team member would own.

This was an excellent start; however, the challenging work was to come as each guiding coalition member had to model these tight expectations in all he or she said, did, and expected at the school level. It was important for Superintendent Murdock and her team to consistently communicate and build a shared understanding of the expectations. They shared their work before teachers left in May of the previous school year and revisited it when teachers returned in the fall. However, this would not be enough, as continuously *leading by doing* would need to continue all year to build capacity and show others what would lead to change. As the school year continued to evolve, some days were easier than others. There were roadblocks Superintendent Murdock would have to overcome personally. There were challenges that would cause leaders at the school level to need time to reflect and revisit the priorities and expectations. It is a continuous work in progress to lead from within by modeling non-negotiable expectations.

Leaders who can carry forward consistent actions that tightly align to their expectations create synergy, and others follow. The next steps for the Lee County guiding coalition included developing a progress-monitoring tool. Members would need to collect or share artifacts to demonstrate how their actions align to the ten tight expectations. A self-monitoring tool is as helpful as it is necessary to hold yourself (and others) accountable for what you plan to do. Moving the plans to action takes real commitment to lead from within. Without accountability, leaders often lose their way and soon find old habits making their way back in their lives. For example, a tight expectation in a school is that all teachers meet twice a week in collaborative teams. The principal starts the year by attending each collaborative team meeting, and gradually as the busy weeks continue, he struggles to maintain any commitment to the teams in his schedule. Before long, he finds himself spending more and more time on tasks and paperwork in his office during the collaborative team meeting times. At the end of the month, the guiding coalition meets to review its actions and artifacts that account for the tight expectations. The principal recognizes that he needs to find some time in his daily schedule to prioritize collaborative teams. Modeling expectations is a crucial leadership skill to impact change. Consider using a daily time log, such as the one in figure 5.3, to assess your daily focus, and practice with figure 5.4 (page 114) to identify where you want to spend your time and monitor your ability to follow through.

Category	Day One	Day Two	Day Three
Daily Focus	Spending most of my time in classrooms and with collaborative teams	Increasing time in classrooms and with collaborative teams	Increasing time in classrooms and with collaborative teams
Classroom observations	48 minutes	100 minutes	100 minutes
Student discipline	100 minutes	30 minutes	40 minutes
Duties (hall, lunchroom, bus yard supervision, and so on)	150 minutes	150 minutes	150 minutes
District meetings			
Emails and office work	160 minutes	30 minutes	45 minutes
Collaborative team meetings		60 minutes	30 minutes
Community engagement		60 minutes	

Source: Spiller & Power, 2019, p. 14.

FIGURE 5.3: Sample daily time log.

continued ➔

Category	Day One	Day Two	Day Three
Human resources			15 minutes
Other		150 minutes	150 minutes

*Visit **go.SolutionTree.com/PLCbooks** for a free reproducible version of this figure.*

Directions: Use the following five-point scale to self-assess your focus on priorities.

1. I am totally distracted from this priority and recognize I have not created a simplistic way for others to understand this focus.

2. I struggle some days with staying focused on this and believe others are not always sure this is a focus.

3. I speak about this priority often and have set up structures and systems that help others understand this work. However, my daily actions are not always aligned with this priority.

4. I believe most days my actions and messages represent the simplicity of what I want to accomplish at this school. However, there are times I do allow distractors to get in the way.

5. I am strongly aligning all of my actions and messages so it is simple for others to understand this is a priority.

Priorities	Score and reflection	What actions can I take to increase my focus and simplify the direction if necessary?
Priority one	I give myself a score of _____ because	
Priority two	I give myself a score of _____ because	
Priority three	I give myself a score of _____ because	

Source: Spiller & Power, 2019, p. 20.

FIGURE 5.4: Assessment tool for simplifying focus and actions in daily practice.

*Visit **go.SolutionTree.com/PLCbooks** for a free reproducible version of this figure.*

Ignoring Seeds of Doubt

Confidence—even when you don't feel it, you need it. Leading from within and staying the course despite all that is happening require you to ignore the seeds of doubt that creep into your thinking. How do they get there in the first place? We classify these doubts in two ways: (1) unintentionally finding their way to your thoughts and (2) intentionally making their way to you. Consider the unintentional negative thoughts that come and go in your mind about so many things. You know it is healthier and best for you to lead with positive intent, believe in good things only, and focus your time and energy on building from purposeful and positive actions. Perhaps you are predisposed to being a "cup-half-empty" person rather than a "cup-half-full" person. You know it is a much stronger position to lead with confidence and positivity, but it is a natural challenge. If this is your personality, it will take intentional effort to move toward a growth mindset. To lead from within and create the changes you wish to make, you must find ways to have intentional confidence and a positive attitude rather than letting the seeds of doubt cloud your thinking, actions, and leadership style. Those you wish to influence and impact will enjoy working with you more when you show a confident, positive outlook.

During our coaching, we find leaders often want a quick fix, a magic potion that can help them stay positive. We know there is much research on the growth mindset (see Duckworth, Dweck, Hanselman, Walton, and Yeager, to name a few), and we have also witnessed very negative leaders intentionally change their focus. It takes determination and a desire to hear and see yourself differently. It takes self-talk and continuous reflection. Purposefully seeing the excellent skills you have and knowing you can move forward confidently can take time. However, you can remove those unintentional seeds of doubt with personal commitment and determination. Use figure 5.5 to self-reflect on ways to grow a positive mindset.

Strategies for Growing a Positive Mindset	Notes and Next Steps
Embrace challenges as opportunities. For example: Change your vocabulary from viewing something as a problem to a challenge or an opportunity. Remind yourself to be solution focused whenever you are straying from this positive intent.	

FIGURE 5.5: Self-reflection to avoid unintentional seeds of doubt.

continued ➡

Strategies for Growing a Positive Mindset	Notes and Next Steps
Focus on the process, not the outcome. For example: Plan the work needed and take it one step, one day, or one moment at a time. Feel the sense of accomplishment as you scaffold the tasks and responsibilities, rather than being overwhelmed by the big picture.	
Celebrate the small wins and notice change. For example: Take a breath and reflect. Notice the small advances you are making in your work; see the changes that are happening. Celebrate personally or with others (whichever feels best).	
Learn what you need to know. For example: Identify the leadership skills you need to continuously build, learn, and practice to build confidence in your abilities. Study what you need to study as a continuous learner.	
Tell yourself a different story. For example: Self-talk is vital to stay focused and positive. Create positive stories, and seek opportunities to rewrite the story so it positively impacts your thinking.	
Surround yourself with growth mindset support. For example: Build shared leadership and understanding with others who can support you and have positive energy. Surround yourself with those who build your confidence.	

Visit **go.SolutionTree.com/PLCbooks** *for a free reproducible version of this figure.*

Now, let's turn to what we consider *intentional* seeds of doubt. In our experiences, others who may want to see you fail or sabotage your leadership plant these seeds of doubt. Unfortunately, it happens. When you accept a leadership position, you have crossed a line others may resent or be jealous of. Or in some cases, because you are on the road to school or district improvement, you are asking people to move out of their comfort zones and do different work, and you are challenging the status quo. The *doubters* try to plant seeds of doubt in your mind about your leadership skills or plans. When this happens to you, leading from within and staying the course will require great strength and character. It is most vital that you focus on your priorities and not let these doubts distract you. Easier said than done? Yes, we know, but very possible. We both had this experience more than once, and it does take great patience and focus. The first step is to recognize when it is happening. This may require time and an honest reflection. Who are your faithful supporters, friends, and coworkers? What might be their intentions? Are the intentions real and helpful? Do their suggestions make sense, or are they primarily complaints? Do they have a history of causing issues? Are you helping plant the seeds of doubt because you are a cup-half-empty person? Are others trying to protect you and advise you, but you are not truly seeing who they are? Once you recognize the pattern and how it makes you feel, you will respond more positively. Use figure 5.6 to consider strategies that will help you stay focused and robust despite intentional seeds of doubt.

Strategies to Help	Notes and Next Steps
Knowledge: Know your business, work, and purpose. Understand your vision and priorities. Study, learn, and grow.	
Time: Spend your time on the right work. Allow others to see you working on priorities, taking care of business, and maintaining your focus.	
Reflection: Continuously reflect and self-monitor your actions and thoughts to maintain a positive focus. Develop personal strategies for when the seeds of doubt wander in.	

FIGURE 5.6: Strategies for focus and strength to ward off intentional seeds of doubt. continued →

Strategies to Help	Notes and Next Steps
Circle of influence: Surround yourself with support, expertise, common sense, and people who ground you and help you see your purpose. Build shared leadership focused on your vision.	
Confront with facts: Use evidence and facts to address saboteurs. Make it clear you will not tolerate behaviors that get in the way of your tight expectations and priorities. Keep feelings out of the equation by sticking to the facts.	
Presentation: Walk with your head high, a smile on your face, and confidence in your step!	
Other ideas:	

*Visit **go.SolutionTree.com/PLCbooks** for a free reproducible version of this figure.*

Developing a Thick Skin (and Balancing This With Grace and Dignity)

Leadership requires a thick skin. We do not mean you need to be invulnerable; however, you will need to desensitize yourself to comments and opportunities others might make about your leadership style or decisions. Again, some of this will be intentional (as discussed in the previous section), but sometimes it will be just opinion or possibly constructive criticism. Whatever the case, observe your reactions to these situations and begin to make personal changes (if required).

Consider this scenario. A new principal is embarking on school improvement. He develops a guiding coalition to lead the PLC process and create collaborative content-area teams. The new principal is excited for the beginning of the school year and ready to lead changes through an improved culture focused on collaboration, learning, and results. He knows this is the correct work and waits with interest for the teachers to feel the same way! About four weeks into the school year, the principal walks into the faculty lounge and overhears a conversation among the most effective, impactful teachers on staff. They are rock solid, and the principal has so much respect for them. What he hears delivers a devastating blow. The group discusses the speed at which he expects them to change and how difficult the collaborative team process is. They want things to return to normal, so they can just go to their classrooms and shut the door. They know how and what to teach and feel confident they can meet students' needs by themselves. The last comment the principal hears is the group wondering if he will last.

The new principal heads back to his office and closes the door. He feels like a balloon that just lost all of its air. He cannot believe these stellar teachers cannot see the benefits of sharing their expertise with others and learning from one another. They are all members of his guiding coalition, and he was sure they would move the learning forward. The principal knows collaborative work is needed; despite the staff's strengths, student achievement at his school has been very low for years, and changes are warranted.

His first instinct is to pack up and leave (at least for the day, but likely he just wants to leave). The principal's second instinct is to go to the lounge and address the group. Both of these ideas might give him short-term comfort; however, to lead from within and go the extra mile, he must step back, reflect, and consider how to lead with grace and dignity. Developing a thick skin means leaders deal with the situations at hand, but make the situation less about anger, pride, or hurt, and more about what will move the school or district forward.

The principal spends some time reflecting on what he heard and decides to meet with the teachers the following day. He is determined to make the conversation positive and learn more from them about what they need and do not understand, and how he can help. He invites the teachers to meet him for coffee early in the morning and to share what he learned. The principal begins the conversation with an apology for not meeting their needs and understanding their frustrations. He talks about why he accepted the position and what he hoped for their collective vision for the school. The principal tells his guiding coalition team members he wants to learn more from them and leads by asking the following guiding questions he prepared the night before.

1. "What is it about the PLC process and collaborating with others that bothers you?"

2. "Where did I miss opportunities to build shared understanding with you as a guiding coalition member and teacher, and with other teachers?"

3. "How could we build collective capacity together as a leadership team?"

The teachers willingly share that the change feels overwhelming and too much. It still feels like extra planning instead of the planning they already do. They are all leading collaborative team discussions, but are not confident they are doing it correctly. They want more training on establishing norms, facilitating the meetings, and focusing teacher conversations on addressing the four PLC questions. The principal agrees that he hasn't spent time with these lead teachers in thoughtful, strategic training. He needs to use the guiding coalition meeting time to let members practice being leaders and building shared understanding. He now can see it through their lens.

Developing a thick skin and balancing leadership practices with grace and dignity mean staying focused on your vision and holding tight expectations, but seeking first to understand. By demonstrating a genuine interest in their feelings, the principal acknowledged what he heard upset him, but he did it respectfully. Instead of embarrassing the teachers, he showed them grace and dignity and honored them by asking for their help in understanding the next steps. It is a balancing act; leaders must confront the brutal realities while allowing others to learn, grow, and feel empowered.

Reflection

What experience or situation have you dealt with a little less (or a great deal less) thick skin than you wanted? What might you have done differently? How could you build more grace and dignity into your leadership practices?

Creating a Work-Life Balance

This is a tough one. We know. We both have struggled with this over the years. How do you go the extra mile, dig deep, and still have a life? Many find it too challenging and cannot create a work-life balance. They leave the profession or at least their leadership position. We find the most impactful way to find a work-life balance is to emphasize taking care of ourselves. In other words, self-care presents the best opportunity for the balance of work and life to exist.

As the world dealt with COVID-19, the topics of self-care and wellness became more relevant. Leaders (and all staff) in schools and districts met the challenges of multiple direction changes, very long hours, and worries about health and safety. The need to problem solve and critically address issues was heightened for anyone accepting the responsibility to lead. With or without a pandemic, self-care is essential.

How many days in your life are you suffering on the inside but must give your all to provide the leadership others need? Each morning is a new day, and that day is important to the students and adults you serve. Leading from within is especially challenging when you are emotionally drained, dealing with grief and sadness, tired (mentally, physically, or both), and allowing the seeds of doubt to exist in your mind.

In the opening of chapter 12 of his book, *HEART!*, educator, author, speaker, and consultant Timothy D. Kanold (2017) quotes Tom Rath: "If you want to make a difference—not just today, but for many years to come—you need to put your health and energy ahead of all else" (p. 79).

As we have grown on our leadership journeys, we have developed personal strategies to put our health and energy first. (We both admit our practices are not perfect and that we also fail to follow them sometimes.) We value our personal time and space, and we protect what we need. For example, Karen's best days start early and end early. She knows she is at her best when she goes to bed early and doesn't miss the early mornings. She loves the quiet reflection time of the early morning, and she needs that space for thinking and setting herself for the day. When it doesn't happen, she is very aware the day will be challenging for her, and she will need to find more inner strength to stay calm and energized. She also knows when she builds automated routines and removes some of the small decisions in her day, she has more energy for the bigger ones. For example, being a consultant on the road since 2010 has been challenging, but Karen also sets the same routines (where her things are in the hotel room, where she stays, and so on) to keep her energy and focus on the work. Karen tries to ensure her basic needs are met, and she knows this includes lots of water every day and one strong coffee to start her morning. Self-care for Karen includes attention to detail, staying organized, and not procrastinating. The little things have become automated or routine.

Jeanne, however, thrives on her interactions with others and also needs to have time for exercise every day. Both of these values create happiness for her, and she prioritizes them in her life. Jeanne also recognizes that she needs routines more than ever before and tries to stick to those routines no matter what is happening in her life. The challenge for her is finding time each day to decompress, reflect, and learn something new, so she is working on ensuring this time makes its way into her routines. For example, it is relaxing for her to listen to a podcast or read a book, giving her the chance to learn, reflect, and decompress all at the same time.

Another strategy we both use is to consider what brings joy to our lives. *Joy* is an internal feeling, and for each person, joyful feelings come from different values.

As you walk through life, external events, people, and so on, can help you feel happy; however, joy comes from your own experiences with what pleases you and creates warm, comforting feelings within yourself. It is about intentionality—or getting deliberate. Brené Brown (2015), research professor at the University of Houston, host of the *Unlocking Us* and *Dare to Lead* podcasts, and author of *Dare to Lead* and many other books, states:

> When I am flooded with fear and scarcity, I try to call forward joy and sufficiency by acknowledging the fear, then transforming it into gratitude. I say this out loud: "I'm feeling vulnerable. That's okay. . . . We cannot ignore our pain and feel compassion for it at the same time. (p. 19)

Finding joy might mean intentionally waking up and watching a sunrise or noticing the beauty around you. Joy can be the pause and breath you take when needed, or perhaps the conversation at the end of a day with a loved one or the hug you give (even when you need one). It might be learning to ask for what you need or paying forward kind deeds. For each person, joyfulness comes from what he or she values and needs in life.

Consider what routines you can create to build self-care into your work-life balance. Reflect on what brings *you* joy. What values must you honor? How can you adjust daily habits to give you more opportunities to feel centered? Use figure 5.7 to reflect and chart next steps. Include what you need to start doing more of and what you might consider *not* doing anymore.

Reflection: What brings me joy and comfort? What routines, habits, and values make a difference in my work-life balance?	What do I need to start doing?	What do I need to stop doing?
For example: I find joy in walking and reflecting at the end of the day.	*I need to take time for my nightly walks.*	*I need to get off my computer at night and go for my walk.*

FIGURE 5.7: Reflection—next steps for work-life balance.

*Visit **go.SolutionTree.com/PLCbooks** for a free reproducible version of this figure.*

Wrap-Up

The fantastic work of leaders creates synergy with others. Momentum and impact build adrenaline, and many people thrive on these positive feelings for many days. However, to continue to lead from within, it is necessary to intentionally stay focused, build healthy, joyful daily practices, and recognize the need to build confidence and expertise as you move forward. Going the extra mile is a leadership commitment, and most leaders learn by doing. You are strong and will develop the resilience you need. Recognize your strengths and build on them as you lead from within. Consider your practices and your current reality as you use the reflective tool (page 124) to identify your next steps. Chapter 6 (page 127) explores strategies for learning always and from everywhere.

Six-Sentence Summary

Leading from within requires intentionally acknowledging a personal commitment to accept the role and responsibility of leadership. As we coach leaders, we witness an authentic desire to remain focused; however, we also see the struggle that transpires without the grit to endure. Leaders who can carry forward with consistent actions that tightly align to their expectations create synergy, and others follow. Leading from within and staying the course despite all that is happening require you to ignore the seeds of doubt that can creep into your thinking. Developing a thick skin means that leaders deal with the situation at hand, but make it less about anger, pride, or hurt, and more about what will move the school or district forward. We find the most impactful way to balance work and our lives is when we emphasize taking care of ourselves.

Making an Impact in Six: Going the Extra Mile (and Looking After Yourself)

The following six ideas provide opportunities for further reflection and action. We provide three reflections on what great leaders do and avoid doing to gain focus, as well as three considerations for how to make an impact in six minutes, six weeks, and six months to guide your leadership planning and practice.

Thoughtful Leaders Do . . .	Thoughtful Leaders Avoid . . .
1. Find the courage and strength to lead from within, despite the obstacles.	Allowing the distractors and seeds of doubt to change their focus and priorities
Current reality and next steps:	
2. Reaffirm their commitment to doing whatever it takes to lead at all times.	Losing sight of their *why* or the purpose and promise they made to lead
Current reality and next steps:	
3. Intentionally create a work-life balance by practicing personal care.	Leading at all costs, especially when that cost is their individual needs and joy in their lives
Current reality and next steps:	

page 1 of 3

4. What will you do in six minutes to go the extra mile and look after yourself?

For example:

- Intentionally use six minutes at the beginning and end of each day to personally reflect. What is your commitment to leadership? How are your actions aligning with this commitment? What can you do differently to build more purpose into your day?

- In a problematic situation, intentionally pause to consider how you can persevere. What strategies will assist you in finding the grit you need immediately to move forward?

My ideas:

5. What will you do in six weeks to go the extra mile and look after yourself?

For example:

- Use helpful activities, such as those in figures 5.2 (page 111), 5.3 (page 113), and 5.4 (page 114), to develop personal practices that model your expectations and assist you in focusing on the necessary work. Keep a log of your daily actions in support of your priorities. Make note of times when it was difficult for you to lead from within and how you responded.

- Take time to understand the unintentional or intentional seeds of doubt impacting your confidence as a leader. Notice when these doubts appear and how they present to you. Clarify the feeling the doubts create and how this changes your ability to lead. Use figures 5.5 (page 115) and 5.6 (page 117) to manage the seeds of doubt and change your mindset and actions.

My ideas:

6. What will you do in six months to go the extra mile and look after yourself?

For example:

- Continue to be intentionally aware of situations you must confront or manage to move forward. Notice when you handle a situation with grace and dignity, and understand how impactful it is when you do this. Create every opportunity to develop habits that assist you in leading from within. Keep a journal or use a graphic organizer to self-monitor your intentional focus on maintaining a thick skin with a balance of grace and dignity.

- Use figure 5.7 (page 122) to understand what brings you joy and creates more work-life balance. What will you do to develop intentional habits over the next six months? How can you self-monitor and adjust as needed?

My ideas:

Chapter 6

Learning Always and From Everywhere

Leadership and learning are indispensable to each other.

—John F. Kennedy

Leaders who lead from within are constantly seeking information that will allow them to deepen their understanding of leadership and what it takes to lead well. They are always searching for ways to improve and seeking lessons on leadership from everywhere they possibly can. Let's define the words *always* and *everywhere* a bit further.

We define the word *always* with these synonyms: *continually, consistently, constantly, eternally, forever, perpetually,* and *24-7.* Leadership lessons are all around you in your day-to-day interactions, in the news, in your observations of students, in the actions of other leaders, and in the responses you witness to your leadership. The lessons are there, and you must be willing to use them as *learning opportunities*—chances to improve and grow your leadership skills regardless of how long you have been leading or how successful you are. Simon Sinek, author and inspirational speaker, describes how great leaders are those who consider themselves students regardless of their status (as cited in Jean-Louis & Rozenbaum, n.d.). Sinek says he knows several experienced, highly respected leaders who constantly read about leadership, talk about leadership, and generally have an insatiable desire to grow as leaders and improve their leadership skills. Sinek adds that these leaders recognize this is a skill they will need to keep working on *forever* (as cited in Jean-Louis & Rozenbaum, n.d.).

This leads to our definition of the word *everywhere*. To us, *everywhere* represents learning from all places and in all contexts. Most definitely, we first look to the experts in the field of educational leadership, as they have expertise and experiences to learn from; in fact, this book references many of them. We can also look outside education to find examples of outstanding leadership we can apply to educational contexts. For example, the leadership team Jeanne works with constantly seeks to understand better ways to lead through podcasts, articles, books, and webinars from great business thinkers and leaders. In this chapter, we explore some of these lessons as examples.

In this complex world, we propose it is easier than ever before to be a learner. There are a variety of ways to access learning, depending on your preferences. If you prefer turning the pages of a book, hard copies are available; digital versions exist for those who like to read on a digital device. If you prefer to listen to a book, many books have audio editions often read by the author. There are podcasts, blogs, social media posts, online courses, and other new ways to learn, likely developed since we wrote this chapter. It can feel a little overwhelming as you consider what authors or platforms to pay attention to, how to apply the learning to your context, and what to take action on or put into practice. And, of course, there is learning from experience. Who you work with, who mentors you, and who provides an example through personal contact or even just an observation from afar, afford you opportunities to learn more about leadership. People learn what to do and not to do as they move through their lives. Reflect on your own learning style. Are you a consummate reader? Do you love the opportunities for learning when leaders get together and share experiences? Do conversations with other leaders energize you, or are you more apt to enjoy the audio version of a leadership book? Consider the *three Ps*: pursue, personalize, and practice, as this final chapter provides the space and time for you to consider a commitment to being a lifelong learner through your leadership journey.

The Three Ps: Pursue, Personalize, and Practice

Leaders are often inundated with professional learning opportunities and information about how to improve outcomes for students. We offer the first P, *pursue*, as a strategy for filtering the never-ending influx of information. The second and third Ps of *personalize* and *practice* offer strategies for using the information and learning effectively.

Pursue

Guiding principle: Pursue information that is reliable, useful, compelling, and resonates with you.

Start with information that evidence backs up. Ask what research studies support the thinking others share. Seek experts who have models based on compelling evidence that confirms their assertions. Consider whether or not their thinking resonates with you. Certain experts share their thinking in abstract and esoteric ways, others express their thinking in concrete, simple statements, and some do a little of both. For example, Brown (2015, 2018, 2021) bases her research around courage, vulnerability, shame, and empathy, and is extremely direct, straightforward, and honest in her writing and podcasts. Not only are Brown's topics interesting to Jeanne, but she also appreciates Brown's style. Karen often turns to John Maxwell (2013) and Lencioni (2012) for commonsense, quick, and impactful reminders of leading from within throughout her leadership journey. Sinek's (2019) writing is always in our bookcases. We turn to many thought leaders as educational leaders, including Reeves (2009, 2020), Fullan (2006), DuFour and colleagues (2016), Muhammad (2018), and many others.

No matter whose work you choose, it's meaningful when it creates aha moments and reflection. If you can apply the work to your current situations and it aids your thinking about your own practice, it impacts your ability to lead from within. Consider your pursuit of leadership lessons. Do you have *go-tos*? Are you more apt to look for lessons, or do you find that resources come to you through connections with colleagues or emails that come your way, podcasts, and so on? How do you intentionally become a student of leadership?

Personalize

Guiding principle: Personalize the information by making meaning of it based on your experiences and context.

Reflect on how you can apply the learning in your setting. Will it help you solve a problem you are currently experiencing? Will it help build your leadership capacity or the leadership capacity of others? Will it help you become a more effective leader? Does it help you think differently about how you behave as a leader? A conversation Jeanne had with her brother, Jimmy, illustrates the idea of personalizing information. Jimmy is the chief executive officer of a company in North Carolina. When Jeanne visits with him, they often discuss leadership. They discussed and agreed that the ideal or preferred method for achieving a goal is through strong partnerships or collaboration. He shared that while this is true, we must also be prepared to achieve the goal when the collaborative process breaks down. As a CEO, he has found that breakdowns in collaboration can be used as an excuse for failure to achieve the goal, so there must be a plan to go over or around the obstacles (in this case the breakdown of the collaborative process) in order to ensure that the goal is reached. The idea is that when the collaborating parties understand that reaching the goal is the ultimate focus, and the preferred method for reaching the goal is through partnership or collaboration, but that other methods will be utilized if necessary, they may choose to be more collaborative in the first place.

The strategy clearly associates with a business strategy, so Jeanne had to personalize it in the context of education. She finds it remarkable how the method applied to the world of education with just a little tweaking. In PLCs, collaboration is also the preferred method to get to the desired result of high levels of student achievement, but we must persevere toward that goal while we are building and honing the collaborative process. This means that while we are working to hone the collaborative process, we may need to go over or around those who are not quite willing or able to engage in the collaborative process effectively. Karen has also learned lessons from her brother, Edgar, who owned a company in Canada for over forty years. Early in her administrative career, Karen interviewed Edgar for a master's research paper. When she asked Edgar about his leadership habits, he talked at length about how impactful it was for him to arrive early to the office. Long before the business opened for the day, he would be in his office and take time to reflect, consider his vision, and create the plan that would continue to move the company forward. His *thinking time* provided a haven for him to lead through many challenging years. Intentionally or unintentionally, Karen developed early morning work habits as well. This is her consistent practice, because she feels the most reflective and productive in the early morning.

Practice

Guiding principle: Practice what you learn by using the information to enhance your work. Learn by doing.

An initial way you can practice what you learn is to share with others. When you share what you learn with others, it deepens your understanding, which will be helpful as you consider the actions you will take to put your learning into practice. You have the benefit of hearing different perspectives and insights as you share your understanding of new concepts. After listening to a podcast from a business-oriented author focused on improving meetings, Jeanne shared information about what she learned with one of her colleagues. She was eager to know what his thoughts were about the new learning. She asked, "What do you think about this? Could it work in the educational context? Could it work for us? Do you think it could be helpful as we consider improving the way we approach collaborative meetings?" The ensuing conversation led to more significant insights and thoughts about applying the learning that Jeanne had not previously considered. She felt better about moving the knowledge into practice as a result of this conversation.

Whenever you can, share your learning and gather insights from critical friends. When it is impossible to share your understanding with others in person, ask for feedback electronically, make it part of a virtual meeting agenda specifically scheduled to elicit feedback, or gather thoughts and insights from other educators via social media. If the goal is to turn knowledge into action (and it is), clarity about the knowledge before implementation is critical. In our leadership practice and through coaching other leaders, we find it easy to linger in the reading and discussing phase and never get to the action. In their book, *The Knowing-Doing Gap: How Smart Companies Turn Knowledge Into Action*, professors and business management sages Jeffrey Pfeffer and Robert I. Sutton (2000) offer this advice: "One of our main recommendations is to engage more frequently in thoughtful action. Spend less time just contemplating and talking about organizational problems. Taking action will generate experiences from which you can learn" (p. 6). The *doing* may initially take you out of your comfort zone a bit, and it may require a little vulnerability, but the staff and you will learn how to improve from the experience. When Karen is coaching, she often asks leaders to consider a *25-75 rule*—this is, studying, reflecting, and talking 25 percent of the time, and doing 75 percent of the time. It is too easy to close the door and have great conversations; however, leadership work needs to be done. This doesn't mean you don't take time to reflect and plan based on the evidence you learn; however, leading from within requires action.

Use figure 6.1 (page 132) to consider how you can grow your leadership practices using the three Ps. Reflect and commit to intentional improvement through pursuing, personalizing, and practicing as you lead from within.

The Three Ps	Your Current Reality What are your current practices in each category?	Your Commitment What will you commit to doing in each category as the next steps for intentional improvement?
Pursue		
Personalize		
Practice		

FIGURE 6.1: Using the three Ps to grow leadership practices.

Visit **go.SolutionTree.com/PLCbooks** *for a free reproducible version of this figure.*

The Three Ps and Lessons You Learn From Others

As this chapter states, learning always and from everywhere requires a steadfast commitment to constantly thinking about and applying learning to your situation. For example, consider two great leadership reads like Jim Collins's (2001) *Good to Great: Why Some Companies Make the Leap . . . and Others Don't* and Collins and Jerry I. Porras's (1994) *Built to Last: Successful Habits of Visionary Companies.* We go back to both books time and time again. Why would these business books be so impactful for two educational leaders? Undoubtedly, the first time we read them we likely saw some truths needed in our leadership journeys. Over the years, as we re-read, we find other, more meaningful and necessary truths at the exact times we pursue this learning. We both personalize the lessons from Collins, and we both see different value in what we read, depending on when and where we need it. In this next section, we create an illustration of the three Ps (pursue, personalize, and practice) using Collins's (2001) level 5 leadership research.

In our coaching work, we often discover we need a way to describe the elements of leadership in a clear, concise manner, especially when working with new leaders. Knowing where to start the pursuit is daunting, as the leadership theories and methods to choose from are extensive and diverse. We always consider the research-based work we know resonates with us—Collins (2001). His research is extensive, his style is crisp, clear, and straightforward, and we both use his framework for leadership to guide our thinking as leaders. Collins's (2001) theory of level 5 leadership was born from the research that led to his book *Good to Great: Why Some Companies Make the Leap . . . and Others Don't*. Collins (2001) set out to answer the question, Can a good company become a great company, and if so, how? The research spans from 1996 to 2000 and includes an extensive exploration of what makes some companies great. Collins (2001) synthesizes the results to identify the drivers of good-to-great transformations. One driver is level 5 leadership, and it made it into the framework as one of the most substantial and consistent contrasts between the good-to-great and comparison companies. With this fascinating information, we further explored the concept to determine if it would be beneficial in working with educational leaders. Some of what we learned was surprising, but it was also compelling and applicable to our work in schools and districts. Here's what we learned.

Defining Level 5 Leadership

What surprised us first is that Collins (2001) was not looking for leadership as a factor in what made some companies great. In fact, he initially tried to downplay the role of executives, but couldn't continue because the research uncovered that each of the good-to-great companies had a rather unusual leader at the helm—a fact Collins (2001) could not ignore. This led to the surprising characteristics each of these leaders share. According to Collins (2001), "level 5 leaders are a study in duality: modest and willful, shy and fearless" (p. 17). We often think about the gregarious, outspoken, and intense leadership style of people like Steve Ballmer, the chief executive officer of Microsoft from 2000 to 2014. An extremely extroverted leader, Ballmer was the unequivocal voice of Microsoft for many years. He was successful and dynamic, but not quite the model of the type of leader Collins (2001) finds helps certain companies make the leap from good to great. Instead, the research says frequently that the successful leaders have a combination of personal humility and professional will (Collins, 2001). Figure 6.2 (page 134) defines the hierarchy of Collins's (2001) level 5 leadership. Let's use the three Ps to explore the concept further.

The level 5 leader sits on top of a hierarchy of capabilities necessary for transforming an organization from good to great. To become a full-fledged level 5 leader requires an individual possess the capabilities of all the lower levels, plus the special characteristics of level 5.

Level 5: Level 5 Executive

Builds enduring greatness through a paradoxical combination of personal humility plus professional will

Level 4: Effective Leader

Catalyzes commitment to and vigorous pursuit of a clear and compelling vision; stimulates the group to high-performance standards

Level 3: Competent Manager

Organizes people and resources toward the effective and efficient pursuit of predetermined objectives

Level 2: Contributing Team Member

Contributes to the achievement of group objectives; works effectively with others in a group setting

Level 1: Highly Capable Individual

Makes productive contributions through talent, knowledge, skills, and good work habits

Source for levels: Collins, 2001.

FIGURE 6.2: The level 5 hierarchy.

Using the Lessons: Pursue

Consider how to use the Collins's (2001) level 5 hierarchy to pursue your learning and leadership style. What can you apply as you think about moving from level 1 to level 5? Perhaps as a new school administrator, you are somewhere between a 3 and 4? When Collins's (2001) book was published, Karen had just become a superintendent. She had already been a principal for five years and considered herself at a level 3 or 4. As she studied Collins's (2001) work, Karen understood the need to pursue and learn more about what would impact her leadership style to reach level 5 leadership. It meant paying more attention to others, building relationships and trust, and focusing on (and not simply managing) her priorities to lead, truly balancing skill and will. Over time, Karen understood the critical need to be courageous and vulnerable due to the humility of Collins's (2001) research. Karen discovered that leadership is about empowering others, building collective efficacy, and knowing it is more important to "look out the window" to give credit and appreciation than to focus on oneself. Humility creates a need to lead from within and stay focused on what you can impact and do in the present. In her quest to continuously improve her leadership knowledge, attitudes, and skills, Jeanne pursued the work of many leadership authors; the sophisticated simplicity of the level 5 hierarchy compelled her. Simply stated but sophisticated is the message the level 5 hierarchy conveys about leadership. For example, each of the five levels conveys straightforward ideas about what makes an effective leader, but the hierarchy as a whole is more complex in that it is not meant to be a sequential climb toward level 5. Instead, a leader who possesses all of the traits described in levels 1 through 4 and the traits communicated in level 5 defines level 5. This was fascinating to Jeanne because it defied some of her initial beliefs about leadership. The pursuit opened her eyes to a different way of thinking about what makes a great leader.

There are examples of level 5 leadership all around you. Milwaukee Bucks basketball star Giannis Antetokounmpo speaks frankly about ego, pride, and humility:

> When you focus on the past, that is *ego*. When you focus on the future, that is *pride*. When you focus on the present, that is *humility*. It is a skill to stay in the moment. It is an objective, you have a plan, and every day you wake up, you take little steps in the present to get you there. (as cited in Milwaukee Bucks, 2021)

It is incredible how there are lessons and examples everywhere you look. Keep pursuing them in your leadership journey.

Using the Lessons: Personalize

Consider how you can personalize level 5 leadership lessons for your own journey. What level do you primarily work in now? How can you create more opportunities to lead from within by using the levels to advance your leadership? How can you apply the learning to your context? As a lifelong learner, Jeanne always intentionally focuses on personalizing what she reads, studies, or sees others model for lessons. Collins's (2001) levels have helped her throughout her career to become more self-aware of her need to move from a manager to a leader. Sharing this reading with others has created critical conversations and reflection. It might take others to help you personalize the learning; in other words, you may not see your growth potential or be objective enough about how you lead to personally learn from the resources at hand. Use figure 6.3 (page 136) to reflect on the five levels of the leadership hierarchy and your current reality. What can you do to move forward as you lead from within? How can you apply a business model such as this one to educational leadership? How can you use this hierarchy to guide and support your leadership growth?

Level 5 Leadership Hierarchy	Characteristics	Self-Reflection **Next Steps, Notes, and Guiding Questions** How can you personalize this level? What is your current reality? What are the levels of others you work with, and what can you do to impact those levels? What can you do to grow your leadership style or that of others?
Level 5: **Level 5** **Executive**	Builds enduring greatness through a paradoxical combination of personal humility plus professional will	
Level 4: **Effective** **Leader**	Catalyzes commitment to and vigorous pursuit of a clear and compelling vision; stimulates the group to high-performance standards	
Level 3: **Competent** **Manager**	Organizes people and resources toward the effective and persistent pursuit of predetermined objectives	
Level 2: **Contributing** **Team Member**	Contributes to the achievement of group objectives; works effectively with others in a group setting	
Level 1: Highly **Capable** **Individual**	Makes productive contributions through talent, knowledge, skills, and good work habits	

Sources for levels: Collins, 2001; Collins & Porras, 1994.

FIGURE 6.3: Personalizing the level 5 leadership hierarchy for growth and reflection.

*Visit **go.SolutionTree.com/PLCbooks** for a free reproducible version of this figure.*

Using the Lessons: Practice

How do you take the ideas of level 5 leadership and apply them in your practice? Be careful not to fall into the trap of learning and rarely doing. We have worked with leaders who are voracious learners, but who struggle to apply what they learn. These leaders are filled with volumes of knowledge about leadership yet continue to lead the same way year after year. *Learning by doing* is a strong characteristic of leaders who accept the responsibility of leading from within. Throughout this book, we offer suggestions of ways to build courage, grit, and perseverance into your daily conversations and actions. By doing so, you are building your leadership capacity, and it is indeed necessary to practice what you expect. When you think about reading a leadership book or watching a leadership webinar, the lessons are genuinely only lessons when you consider how you will apply them in your daily life. What will you do to try? How will you practice? For example, if you consider yourself at level 3 of Collins's (2001) hierarchy, what can you do to move to level 4 or 5? How could you practice a leadership strategy that will help you move from managing to leading? In what ways could you become less task driven and more focused on building the skills and confidence of others through trust and credibility? How could you model your expectations more frequently? In other words, how do you roll up your sleeves and lead by example? This might be as simple as leading a school collaborative team as it creates a scoring rubric and applies it to student work. In a district office, you might model the use of data as you lead principals in a data discussion. It is about *doing*—not just assigning tasks and delegating. Learning by doing is an excellent example of how others will see you leading through your work. Leading from within requires attention to what and how you do things, not just what you expect of others. Consider ways you can intentionally practice leadership strategies to support your growth toward level 5 leadership.

Reflection

Consider your leadership journey. What lessons from everywhere could you build into your daily practice? How can these lessons help you move toward level 5 leadership?

The Growth of Others

As you grow and learn as a leader, it is crucial to surround yourself with others who want to lead and learn with you. In fact, Collins's (2001) level 5 speaks to the need to build capacity through sharing ownership and celebrating the work of others. In other words, to truly lead from within, you must consider how you are helping others seek learning opportunities always and from everywhere. As previously mentioned, one way to do this is to invite others to share in your learning, seeking every opportunity to engage in learning conversations and open the minds of others to new information, research, and expertise. Allowing others to be personal and practice with you builds both individual and collective capacity.

Great leaders we have worked with allow others around them to shine. They understand that doing so is part of learning together—always and from everywhere as you empower, inspire, and grow individual skills. We have also known leaders who genuinely struggle to let others do the work and take credit for it. Perhaps these leaders feel threatened and are concerned they will lose their influence if they give away their power—or maybe they just do not recognize this is the unintentional impact of their actions. Leading from within requires you to reflect on how you personally manage your power. Do you struggle to share leadership? Are you trying to do everything yourself in fear of being seen as incompetent if you allow others to lead? What holds you back from authentically building capacity? Can you create more opportunities to learn from others close to you and, at the same time, create more opportunities for them to learn from you? Use figure 6.4 to reflect on guiding questions as you honestly consider your shared-leadership skills.

Guiding Questions	Notes and Next Steps
Do you struggle to share leadership? If yes, what is holding you back? If not, write an example that provides evidence of how you currently build shared leadership.	
How can you create more opportunities to learn from others close to you and, at the same time, create more opportunities for them to learn from you?	
Are you trying to do everything yourself in fear of being seen as incompetent if you allow others to lead? If yes, what can you do to change this? If not, how do you know?	

FIGURE 6.4: Reflection—shared leadership.

*Visit **go.SolutionTree.com/PLCbooks** for a free reproducible version of this figure.*

Wrap-Up

In this chapter, we ask you to pursue learning always and from everywhere and use the example of learning from the work of Collins (2001). We also encourage you, as a leader, to learn often and from every experience, person, and interaction. We find ourselves making connections from our daily lives to what we do as educational leaders all the time.

A challenging snowmobiling experience led Jeanne to connect to what she does every day in schools, and how her experience could translate into a tale she could share with others that might remind them about their purpose as educators. The tale includes a thirty-mile snowmobile trek through the mountains of Wyoming to the remote cabin (only accessible by snowmobile) that would be her home for three days. Let's just say this journey was a challenge for Jeanne, as this was her first time snowmobiling in the mountains. Her expedition to the cabin included many obstacles, including getting started on the trek a bit later than expected, with impending darkness and the threat of elk, mountain lions, and bears who like to frequent the trail, especially in the dark. Additionally, her snowmobile temperature gauge indicated the engine was close to overheating, which required many stops along the way to pack the engine with snow to cool it down. The dialogue in Jeanne's mind throughout the trip was, "You need to get to the cabin; keep going, you can do it." She also wished someone would just move the cabin closer to save her from the struggle to get there. It sounds a little bit like what happens in education, doesn't it?

Educators' goal is to get all students to the cabin, which represents high levels (grade level or higher) of learning for all. Jeanne had to overcome obstacles along the way to make it to the cabin. Getting all students to high levels of learning is also fraught with challenges, but you must do your best to get them there, no matter what. Others can't make it easier by moving the cabin closer, and if they could, they would take away the opportunity for students to learn at high levels by depriving students of the productive struggle often necessary to succeed in anything. What experiences do you have that illustrate the work you do in education? How can you use those experiences to create a mental model for those you lead? Stories help make ideas stick. What do you want to stick about you as a leader, and what experiences can you draw on to make connections for yourself and for those you lead? Pursue lessons from your experiences, the writing and thinking of others, and the models that surround you every day. Personalize the lessons so they make sense to you, and then put those ideas that resonate most into your practice as soon as you can. Use the reflective tool (page 141) to identify your next steps.

Six-Sentence Summary

Leaders who lead from within are constantly seeking information to deepen their understanding of leadership and what it takes to lead well. Leadership lessons are all around you in your day-to-day interactions, in the news, in your observations of students, in the actions of other leaders, and in the responses you witness to your own leadership. Think about how you can use these experiences to guide your leadership practice. Consider the three guiding principles of pursue, personalize, and practice to advance your leadership journey: pursue reliable, useful, and compelling information that resonates with you; personalize the information by making meaning of it based on your experiences and context; and practice what you learn by using the information to enhance your work. As you grow and learn as a leader, it is essential to surround yourself with others who want to lead and learn with you. Share what you learn with others to solidify your understanding and possibly new ways of thinking about what you are learning.

Making an Impact in Six: Learning Always and From Everywhere

The following six ideas provide opportunities for further reflection and action. We provide three reflections on what great leaders do and avoid doing to gain focus, as well as three considerations for how to make an impact in six minutes, six weeks, and six months to guide your leadership planning and practice.

Thoughtful Leaders Do . . .	Thoughtful Leaders Avoid . . .
1. Understand there are always life lessons everywhere, and are intentionally aware of what they can learn.	Assuming they know all they need to know and are not open to new ideas and different thought leaders
Current reality and next steps:	
2. Consider how to apply the three Ps (pursuing, personalizing, and practicing) to learning moments as lifelong learners.	Ignoring opportunities to learn from business leaders and leading organizations within and outside the educational community
Current reality and next steps:	
3. Recognize when they share learning with others, they gain critical insights and perspectives that may shift their initial thinking about the concept or idea.	Keeping the learning and thinking to themselves to make sense of the teaching in the way they choose, without complicating it further by hearing different perspectives
Current reality and next steps:	

4. What will you do in six minutes to learn always and from everywhere?

For example:

Each week, take six minutes to follow someone new on Twitter, read a tweet, or look for a quote on leadership that resonates with you, and consider how it can be helpful to you in your leadership practice.

My ideas:

5. What will you do in six weeks to learn always and from everywhere?

For example:

Each week for six weeks, consider your weekly interactions and what you learn about leadership from each one. Write down what you learned so you can begin to see how the ordinary can offer powerful lessons about leadership.

My ideas:

6. What will you do in six months to learn always and from everywhere?

For example:

Each month for six months, decide on a monthly focus for new learning. For example, in month one, pursue leadership learning from an author outside the educational world and share your understanding with another leader in your system. In month two, commit to learning by setting up opportunities to observe others leading and reflect with them about their practice. Set up the next four months to intentionally step outside your comfort zone to learn something new in a new way.

My ideas:

Afterword

True leadership comes not from the sound of a commanding voice but from the nudging of an inner voice—from our own realization that the time has come to go beyond dreaming to doing.

—Madeleine Albright

Like "the nudging of an inner voice," leading from within calls educators to listen to this voice, even when a louder, commanding voice may be steering them in a different direction. We urge you to stay connected to your inner voice and lead every day with your values and beliefs firmly intact. We have learned leadership requires intentionality, which is why we wrote our first book together, *Leading With Intention* (Spiller & Power, 2019). You must dig deep inside yourself to lead intentionally from a place that aligns with who you are. In *Leading With Intention*, we remind you that you are the architect, designer, motivator, planner, fixer, builder, creator of futures, and keeper of dreams (Spiller & Power, 2019). You are responsible. You have an impact. *You are a leader.* We remind you again of the great responsibility and power you have as a leader to create a PLC undeniably focused on learning for educators, so all students can learn—no matter what. You are responsible to lead with intention, integrity, and from deep within, even when faced with challenges.

Leadership is hard. *Really hard.* Grueling, exhausting, bewildering, and complicated, just to name a few of the descriptive words that come to mind. On the flip side, it is also rewarding, worthwhile, necessary, and valuable. Recognizing this, we wrote this book to address this complicated dynamic. We know when things are hard, and they will often be, you need to slow down and lead from within your values. We do not mean you must delay every decision until you have taken hours to think each one through. Instead, we ask you to *take a few minutes* to filter your decisions and actions to ensure they fully represent your beliefs, mission, and vision. Think about your behavior and what you are modeling through your actions. How are you behaving when everyone is stressed? Do you bring their shoulders down, or do you escalate the stress? When someone enters your office flustered and anxious, do you slow down and truly listen, seeking to understand, or do you jump to solving the problem before truly understanding the issue? We firmly believe the day-to-day actions that may seem insignificant are what make a difference. Leaders who lead from within work hard to consider their daily actions and whether or not they model what they expect of others.

We hope the ideas and opportunities for self-reflection we provide in this book serve as a guide as you work to lead from within. In the introduction (page 1), we shared why we offered six chapters and reflected on the significance of the number *six*. We described the number six as the symbol of luck, highest number on a die, and symbol of Venus, the goddess of love. Having a *sixth sense* refers to extrasensory perception (ESP). It is also common to hear someone using the phrase *the sixth sense* when meaning a hunch or instinct. We think it is important to reiterate we know leading from within will require some sixth sense as you learn to understand yourself and others, and develop your own capacity to trust your instincts to make decisions.

None of this is easy. In fact, we are both still working on living the ideas we share with you in our own practice every single day—we are far from "there" yet. We both constantly work on improving our leadership practices, even though Karen retired from a formal leadership role in 2013, and Jeanne is closing in on her last few years before retiring from a formal leadership role. We still sometimes act impulsively or model behaviors we are not necessarily proud of, but we keep working on it and try to be better each time. We keep listening to our inner voice, even when it's not easy to do so.

We leave you with a quote from Theodore Roosevelt (as cited in McCarthy, 2015) that guides the work of author Brown (2015, 2018), who we reference in chapter 1 (page 9). This quote embodies the idea that you should keep getting in the arena even though you know it will be hard and you might fail. When you do fail, get up, dust yourself off, and get right back in the arena! This is what we believe intentional, thoughtful leaders do. How can you apply this quote to what you do as a leader every day?

Roosevelt says:

> It is not the critic who counts; not the man who points out how the strong man stumbles, or where the doer of deeds could have done them better. The credit belongs to the man who is actually in the arena, whose face is marred by dust and sweat and blood; who strives valiantly; who errs, who comes short again and again, because there is no effort without error and shortcoming; but who does actually strive to do the deeds; who knows great enthusiasms, the great devotions; who spends himself in a worthy cause; who at the best knows in the end the triumph of high achievement, and who at the worst, if he fails, at least fails while daring greatly, so that his place shall never be with those cold and timid souls who neither know victory nor defeat. (as cited in McCarthy, 2015)

We invite you to trust your inner voice as you get in the arena. Your leadership matters. Be intentional and lead from within.

References and Resources

Ambrose, D. (1987). *Managing complex change*. Pittsburgh, PA: Enterprise.

BBC News. (2020). *Coronavirus: How New Zealand relied on science and empathy*. Accessed at www.bbc.com/news/world-asia-52344299 on April 1, 2022.

Bloom, G., Castagna, C., Moir, E., & Warren, B. (2005). *Blended coaching: Skills and strategies to support principal development*. Thousand Oaks, CA: Corwin Press.

BrainyQuote. (n.d.). *Rosalynn Carter quotes*. Accessed at https://brainyquote.com/quotes /rosalynn_carter_126340#:~:text=Rosalynn%20Carter%20Quotes&text=A%20 leader%20takes%20people%20where%20they%20want%20to%20go.,go%2C%20 but%20ought%20to%20be on December 7, 2021.

Brave. (n.d.). In *Merriam-Webster's online dictionary*. Accessed at https://merriam-webster .com/dictionary/brave on December 3, 2021.

Broom, A. (Host). (2021). 2-point vs 3-point communication [Audio podcast]. In *Michael Grinder & Associates*. Accessed at https://michaelgrinder.com/2-point-vs-3-point -communication on December 6, 2021.

Brown, B. (2015). *Daring greatly: How the courage to be vulnerable transforms the way we live, love, parent, and lead*. New York: Penguin Random House.

Brown, B. (2018). *Dare to lead: Brave work. Tough conversations. Whole hearts.* New York: Penguin Random House.

Brown, B. (2021). *Dare to Lead hub*. Accessed at https://daretolead.brenebrown.com on December 10, 2021.

Buffum, A., Mattos, M., & Malone, J. (2018). *Taking action: A handbook for RTI at Work*. Bloomington, IN: Solution Tree Press.

Campbell., J., & van Nieuwerburgh, C. (2018). *The leader's guide to coaching in schools: Creating conditions for effective learning*. Thousand Oaks, CA: Corwin Press.

Christman, J. B., Neild, R. C., Bulkley, K., Blanc, S., Liu, R., Mitchell, C., et al. (2009). *Making the most of interim assessment data: Lessons from Philadelphia*. Philadelphia: Research for Action. Accessed at https://researchgate.net/publication/277731833 _Making_the_Most_of_Interim_Assessment_Data_Lessons_from_Philadelphia /link/557ee5f508aeb61eae260e77/download on December 1, 2021.

Collins, J. (2001). *Good to great: Why some companies make the leap . . . and others don't.* New York: HarperBusiness.

Collins, J., & Porras, J. I. (1994). *Built to last: Successful habits of visionary companies.* New York: HarperBusiness.

Conzemius, A. E., & O'Neill, J. (2014). *The handbook for SMART school teams: Revitalizing best practices for collaboration* (2nd ed.). Bloomington, IN: Solution Tree Press.

Croce, J. (1972). Time in a bottle [Recorded by Jim Croce]. On *You don't mess around with Jim* [CD]. New York: ABC.

Cunningham, L. (2013, March 29). *Decision making for the indecisive* [Blog post]. Accessed at www.washingtonpost.com/national/on-leadership/decision-making-for-the-indecisive/2013/03/28/9d8290f6-9692-11e2-9e23-09dce87f75a1_story.html on March 23, 2021.

Davis, K. (2018). *Brave leadership: Unleash your most confident, powerful, and authentic self to get the results you need.* Austin, TX: Greenleaf Book Group Press.

Duckworth, A. (2016). *Grit: The power of passion and perseverance.* New York: Simon & Schuster.

DuFour, R., DuFour, R., Eaker, R., Many, T. W., & Mattos, M. (2016). *Learning by doing: A handbook for Professional Learning Communities at Work* (3rd ed.). Bloomington, IN: Solution Tree Press.

Eaker, R. (2020). *A summing up: Teaching and learning in effective schools and PLCs at Work.* Bloomington, IN: Solution Tree Press.

Fullan, M. (2006, November). *Change theory: A force for school improvement* (Seminar Series Paper No. 157). Jolimont, Victoria, Australia: Centre for Strategic Education. Accessed at http://michaelfullan.ca/wp-content/uploads/2016/06/13396072630.pdf on December 9, 2021.

Galofaro, C. (2021, July 29). Simone Biles told her replacement to "have fun," and she did. *Associated Press.* Accessed at https://apnews.com/article/2020-tokyo-olympics-gymnastics-simone-biles-jade-carey-d6df4be57a8bab145e87160eb8fff892 on December 3, 2021.

Garmston, R., & Wellman, B. (2016). *The adaptive school: A sourcebook for developing collaborative groups* (3rd ed.). Lanham, MD: Rowman & Littlefield.

Glanz, J. (2002). *Finding your leadership style: A guide for educators.* Alexandria, VA: Association for Supervision and Curriculum Development.

Goleman, D. (2000, March–April). Leadership that gets results. *Harvard Business Review.* Accessed at https://hbr.org/2000/03/leadership-that-gets-results on December 3, 2021.

Grant, A. (2021). *Think again: The power of knowing what you don't know.* New York: Viking.

Gruenert, S., & Whitaker, T. (2015). *School culture rewired: How to define, assess, and transform it*. Alexandria, VA: Association for Supervision and Curriculum Development.

Harris, S. (2016). *Bravo principal! Building relationships with actions that value others* (2nd ed.). New York: Routledge.

Heath, C., & Heath, D. (2013). *Decisive: How to make better choices in life and work*. New York: Random House.

Heath, D. (2020). *Upstream: The quest to solve problems before they happen*. New York: Avid Reader Press.

Intrator, S. M., & Scribner, M. (Eds.). (2007). *Leading from within: Poetry that sustains the courage to lead*. San Francisco: Jossey-Boss.

Jean-Louis, J., & Rozenbaum, A. (n.d.). *Want to become a great leader? Act like a student, not an expert* [Video file]. Accessed at https://inc.com/video/simon-sinek/how-good -leaders-become-great.html on December 3, 2021.

Kanold, T. D. (2017). *HEART! Fully forming your professional life as a teacher and leader*. Bloomington, IN: Solution Tree Press.

Killion, J. (2008, February). *Coaches help mine the data*. Accessed at https://learning forward.org/wp-content/uploads/2008/02/focus-on-nsdc-standards.pdf on December 17, 2021.

Kintner-Duffy, V. (2017, February 15). *A coaching guide to asking reflective questions* [Blog post]. Accessed at http://info.teachstone.com/blog/a-coaching-guide-to-asking -reflective-questions-part-1 on December 2, 2021.

Kotter, J. P. (2008). *A sense of urgency*. Boston: Harvard Business School Publishing.

Kotter, J. P. (2012). *Leading change*. Boston: Harvard Business Review Press.

Lencioni, P. (2012). *The advantage: Why organizational health trumps everything else in business*. Hoboken, NJ: Wiley.

Lipton, L., & Wellman, B. M. (2003). *Mentoring matters: A practical guide to learning-focused relationships* (2nd ed.). Charlotte, VT: MiraVia.

Lipton, L., & Wellman, B. M. (2017). *Mentoring matters: A practical guide to learning-focused relationships* (3rd ed.). Charlotte, VT: MiraVia.

Many, T. (2009, March/April). Three rules help manage assessment data. *TEPSA News, 66*(2), 7–8. Accessed at https://absenterprisedotcom.files.wordpress.com/2016/06 /many_tepsa_datarules90.pdf on January 6, 2021.

Maxwell, J. C. (2013). The 5 *Levels of leadership: Proven steps to maximize your potential*. Nashville, TN: Center Street.

McCarthy, E. (2015). *Roosevelt's "The man in the arena."* Accessed at https://mentalfloss .com/article/63389/roosevelts-man-arena on December 15, 2021.

Milwaukee Bucks. (2021, July 17). *"When you focus on the past, that's your ego." Giannis Antetokounmpo life lessons* [Video file]. Accessed at www.youtube.com /watch?v=-qLchg4xkOY on December 3, 2021.

Muhammad, A. (2018). *Transforming school culture: How to overcome staff division* (2nd ed.). Bloomington, IN: Solution Tree Press.

Muhammad, A., & Cruz, L. F. (2019). *Time for change: Four essential skills for transformational school and district leaders.* Bloomington, IN: Solution Tree Press.

MysticalNumbers.com. (n.d.). *Number 6.* Accessed at https://mysticalnumbers.com /number-6 on April 1, 2022.

Needham, K. (2022). *New Zealand PM Jacinda Ardern cancels her wedding amid new Omicron restrictions.* Accessed at www.reuters.com/world/asia-pacific/new-zealand -impose-restrictions-after-omicron-community-spread-2022-01-22 on April 1, 2022.

New Zealand Ministry of Health. (2021). *COVID-19: Current cases.* Accessed at https://health.govt.nz/our-work/diseases-and-conditions/covid-19-novel-coronavirus /covid-19-data-and-statistics/covid-19-current-cases#current-situation on December 2, 2021.

O'Neill, J., & Conzemius, A. E. (2006). *The power of SMART goals: Using goals to improve student learning.* Bloomington, IN: Solution Tree Press.

Patterson, K., Grenny, J., McMillan, R., & Switzler, A. (2012). *Crucial conversations: Tools for talking when stakes are high* (2nd ed.). New York: McGraw-Hill.

Pfeffer, J., & Sutton, R. I. (2000). *The knowing-doing gap: How smart companies turn knowledge into action.* Boston: Harvard Business School Publishing.

Press Association. (1989, May 3). *Margaret Thatcher: Interview for Press Association (10th anniversary as prime minister).* Accessed at https://margaretthatcher.org /document/107427 on December 6, 2021.

Reeves, D. (2009). *Leading change in your school: How to conquer myths, build commitment, and get results.* Alexandria, VA: Association for Supervision and Curriculum Development.

Reeves, D. (2020). *Achieving equity and excellence: Immediate results from the lessons of high-poverty, high-success schools.* Bloomington, IN: Solution Tree Press.

Riegel, D. B. (2018). Why the most successful leaders don't care about being liked. *The Boda Group.* Accessed at www.bodagroup.com/2018/11/01/why-the-most -successful-leaders-dont-care-about-being-liked on December 2, 2021.

Schottey, M. (2013, January 11). Pete Carroll shares the Seahawks' winning philosophy with *Bleacher Report. Bleacher Report.* Accessed at https://bleacherreport.com /articles/1480332-pete-carroll-shares-the-seahawks-winning-philosophy-with -bleacher-report on December 1, 2021.

Senge, P. M. (2006). *The fifth discipline: The art and practice of the learning organization* (Rev. & updated ed.). Redfern, New South Wales, Australia: Currency Press.

Sinek, S. (2019). *The infinite game.* New York: Portfolio/Penguin.

Spiller, J., & Power, K. (2019). *Leading with intention: Eight areas for reflection and planning in your PLC at Work.* Bloomington, IN: Solution Tree Press.

Stanier, M. B. (2016). *The coaching habit: Say less, ask more and change the way you lead forever.* Toronto, Ontario, Canada: Box of Crayons.

Tardanico, S. (2013, January 15). 10 traits of courageous leaders. *Forbes.* Accessed at www.forbes.com/sites/susantardanico/2013/01/15/10-traits-of-courageous -leaders/?sh=5f576e154fc0 on December 2, 2021.

Taylor, S. J. (2018, January 8). *Three reasons why Oprah has a beautiful brain* [Blog post]. Accessed at https://shontejtaylor.com/brain-leadership-blog/2018/1/8/3-reasons-why -oprah-has-a-beautiful-brain on December 3, 2021.

Turkle, S. (2015). *Reclaiming conversation: The power of talk in the digital age.* New York: Penguin Press.

Whitmore, J. (2017). *Coaching for performance: The principles and practice of coaching and leadership* (5th ed.). London: Brealey.

Index

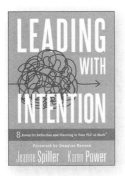

Leading With Intention
Jeanne Spiller and Karen Power
Designed as a guide and reflective tool, *Leading With Intention* will help focus your invaluable everyday work as a school leader. Discover actionable steps for creating a highly effective school community in which staff collaborate, make evidence-based decisions, and believe students are the top priority.
BKF829

Help Your Team
Michael D. Bayewitz, Scott A. Cunningham, Joseph A. Ianora, Brandon Jones, Maria Nielsen, Will Remmert, Bob Sonju, and Jeanne Spiller
Written by eight PLC at Work experts, this practical guide addresses the most common challenges facing collaborative teams. Each chapter offers a variety of templates, processes, and strategies to help your team resolve conflict, focus on the right work, and take collective responsibility for student success.
BKF886

Formative Tools for Leaders in a PLC at Work
Kim Bailey and Chris Jakicic
Learn, do, and lead with the guidance of *Formative Tools for Leaders in a PLC at Work*. With this practical resource, you'll discover how to gather evidence from staff, use that evidence to gauge your PLC's effectiveness, and then make targeted decisions about next steps for improvement.
BKF990

Make It Happen
Kim Bailey and Chris Jakicic
Ensure every team is engaged in the right work with a collective focus on improved student learning. Aligned to the Professional Learning Communities (PLC) at Work model, this resource includes processes, protocols, templates, and strategies designed to support the multidimensional work of instructional coaches.
BKF840

Solution Tree | Press
a division of

Solution Tree

Visit SolutionTree.com or call 800.733.6786 to order.